The Mathematics of
TRADES AND
PROFESSIONS

Table of Contents

Mathematics of Trades and Professions, SV 9780547625560

Part III: Other Professions

Support Materials

Introduction

The **Consumer Math** series is designed to help consumers understand mathematics as it relates to their everyday lives. Activities in this series help students not only understand the underlying mathematical concepts and equations they encounter day to day, but also helps them to be more financially savvy.

Each workbook in the series is divided into three sections and begins with a basic review of math concepts before moving on to more specific topics. Each section includes the following: Pre-Skills Test, Problem Solving Strategies, a Review, and a Test.

In addition, each workbook includes the following support material: Group projects, Practice forms, Charts, a Glossary, and an Answer Key.

The Mathematics of Trades and Professions

The Mathematics of Trades and Professions covers many of the principles of math that are faced daily in the workplace. Part I serves as a basic review of fundamental math concepts. Part II focuses on trades that traditionally involve construction, such as carpentry, plumbing, and masonry. Part III concentrates on concepts and applications needed for such careers as advertising, sales, and nursing.

Part I: Math Skills and Concepts
- Whole Numbers
- Fractions, Decimals, & Percents
- Mean, Median, & Mode
- Basic Operations on a Calculator
- Computing Mentally
- Estimating

Part II: Trade Industries
- Carpentry
- Plumbing
- Electrical Contracting
- Painting
- Masonry
- Money Tips

Part III: Other Professions
- Advertising
- Sales
- Travel
- Manufacturing
- Health Care
- Communications
- Money Tips

Comprehensive Lessons

A **Pre-Skills Test** preceding each section helps teachers evaluate students' abilities and determine learning needs before beginning the lessons.

A wide variety of relevant exercises and activities engage students and keep them interested. Examples are motivated through real-world applications. Exercises include individual skills practice, mixed practice, and application problems.

Extension features offer more challenging problems related to the lesson's theme. **Calculator** activities present problems in which using a calculator is advantageous over paper and pencil. Interesting, real-life problems in **Think About It** spur class participation and provide additional opportunities to assess students' understanding.

Focused review and assessment opportunities are also included for each section.

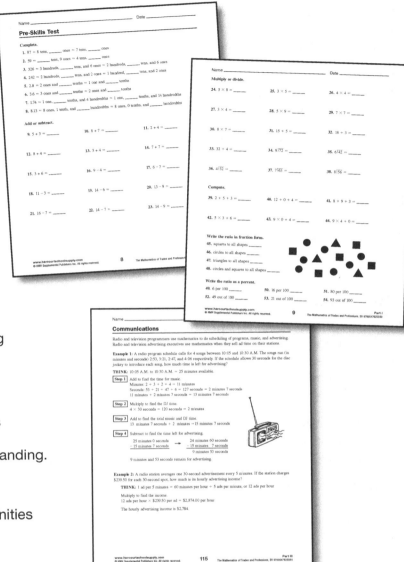

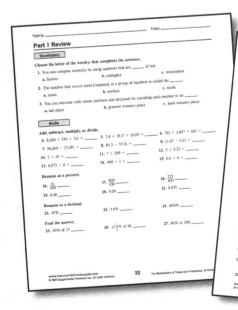

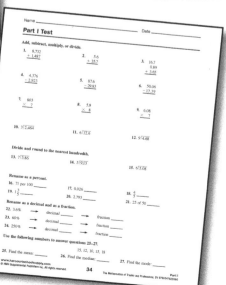

Extension Features

Money Tips examines the practical issues that affect buying decisions. Students look at factors that influence the cost of consumer goods as well as those that create consumer demand.

Mental Math helps students develop techniques to solve problems without using paper and pencil while reinforcing their confidence and estimation skills.

Estimation Skills extends students' understanding of estimation techniques and underscores their utility and practicality.

Calculator activities teach the keys and functions commonly available on calculators and emphasize the time-saving benefits.

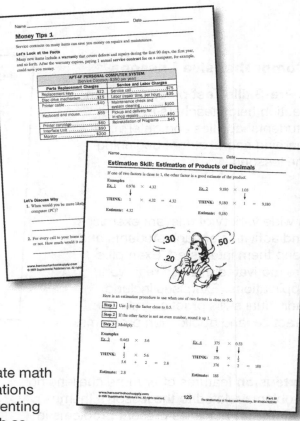

A Strong Base in Problem Solving

Multiple **Problem Solving Applications** in each book relate math skills to people, careers, and the world around us. Applications throughout the series address consumer topics, such as renting apartments and finding miles per gallon, and careers, such as pharmacist and carpenter, which require the use of math skills.

Each **Problem Solving Strategy** presents a realistic problem, a strategy, and a step-by-step approach to solving the problem. Practice exercises reinforce the strategy. Strategies include Drawing a Diagram, Using Estimation, Using a Map, and Working Backward.

Decision Making features offer open-ended lessons that reinforce logical reasoning and move beyond computation to a consideration of factors involved in making sound decisions. Lessons in the *Consumer Math* series include Choosing Transportation, Developing a Budget, Buying Stocks, and Choosing the Correct Tax Form.

Support Materials

Group Projects

Practice Forms

Charts

Glossary

Answer Key

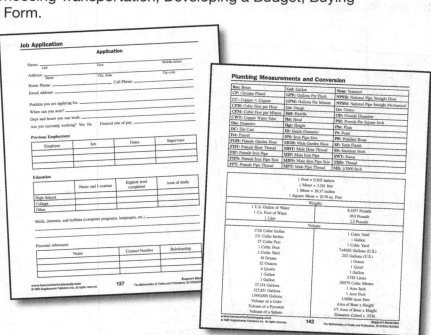

Part I:
Math Skills and Concepts

Pre-Skills Test

Complete.

1. 87 = 8 tens, _____ ones = 7 tens, _____ ones

2. 59 = _____ tens, 9 ones = 4 tens, _____ ones

3. 326 = 3 hundreds, _____ tens, and 6 ones = 2 hundreds, _____ tens, and 6 ones

4. 242 = 2 hundreds, _____ tens, and 2 ones = 1 hundred, _____ tens, and 2 ones

5. 2.8 = 2 ones and _____ tenths = 1 one and _____ tenths

6. 3.6 = 3 ones and _____ tenths = 2 ones and _____ tenths

7. 1.74 = 1 one, _____ tenths, and 4 hundredths = 1 one, _____ tenths, and 14 hundredths

8. 8.13 = 8 ones, 1 tenth, and _____ hundredths = 8 ones, 0 tenths, and _____ hundredths

Add or subtract.

9. 5 + 3 = _____

10. 8 + 7 = _____

11. 2 + 4 = _____

12. 8 + 4 = _____

13. 3 + 4 = _____

14. 7 + 7 = _____

15. 3 + 6 = _____

16. 9 − 4 = _____

17. 6 − 3 = _____

18. 11 − 3 = _____

19. 14 − 6 = _____

20. 13 − 9 = _____

21. 16 − 7 = _____

22. 14 − 7 = _____

23. 14 − 9 = _____

Name _____ Date _____

Multiply or divide.

24. $5 \times 8 =$ _____

25. $3 \times 5 =$ _____

26. $4 \times 4 =$ _____

27. $3 \times 4 =$ _____

28. $5 \times 9 =$ _____

29. $7 \times 7 =$ _____

30. $8 \times 7 =$ _____

31. $15 \div 5 =$ _____

32. $18 \div 3 =$ _____

33. $32 \div 4 =$ _____

34. $9\overline{)72} =$ _____

35. $6\overline{)42} =$ _____

36. $4\overline{)32} =$ _____

37. $7\overline{)63} =$ _____

38. $8\overline{)56} =$ _____

Compute.

39. $2 + 5 + 3 =$ _____

40. $12 + 0 + 4 =$ _____

41. $8 + 9 + 3 =$ _____

42. $5 \times 3 + 6 =$ _____

43. $9 \times 0 + 4 =$ _____

44. $9 \times 4 + 0 =$ _____

Write the ratio in fraction form.

45. squares to all shapes _____

46. circles to all shapes _____

47. triangles to all shapes _____

48. circles and squares to all shapes _____

Write the ratio as a percent.

49. 6 per 100 _____

50. 16 per 100 _____

51. 80 per 100 _____

52. 49 out of 100 _____

53. 21 out of 100 _____

54. 93 out of 100 _____

The Mathematics of Trades and Professions, SV 9780547625560

Adding and Subtracting Whole Numbers and Decimals

Addition and subtraction are related operations.

> Addend + Addend = Sum   Sum − Addend = Addend (= Difference)

Skill 1   **Adding or subtracting whole numbers**

(1a) Add 4,068 + 5,794

Step 1	**Step 2**	**Step 3**	**Step 4**
Add ones. Regroup.	Add tens. Regroup.	Add hundreds.	Add thousands.
$\begin{array}{r} 1 \\ 4,068 \\ +\ 5,794 \\ \hline 2 \end{array}$	$\begin{array}{r} 1\ 1 \\ 4,068 \\ +\ 5,794 \\ \hline 62 \end{array}$	$\begin{array}{r} 1\ 1 \\ 4,068 \\ +\ 5,794 \\ \hline 862 \end{array}$	$\begin{array}{r} 1\ 1 \\ 4,068 \\ +\ 5,794 \\ \hline 9,862 \end{array}$

(1b) Subtract 8,674 − 6,319

Step 1	**Step 2**	**Step 3**	**Step 4**
Regroup tens. Subtract ones.	Subtract tens.	Subtract hundreds.	Subtract thousands.
$\begin{array}{r} {}^{6\,14} \\ 8,6\cancel{7}\cancel{4} \\ -\ 6,319 \\ \hline 5 \end{array}$	$\begin{array}{r} {}^{6\,14} \\ 8,6\cancel{7}\cancel{4} \\ -\ 6,319 \\ \hline 55 \end{array}$	$\begin{array}{r} {}^{6\,14} \\ 8,6\cancel{7}\cancel{4} \\ -\ 6,319 \\ \hline 355 \end{array}$	$\begin{array}{r} {}^{6\,14} \\ 8,6\cancel{7}\cancel{4} \\ -\ 6,319 \\ \hline 2,355 \end{array}$

Skill 2   **Respect the position of the decimal point when adding or subtracting.**

Subtract: 9.2 − 0.7

Step 1	**Step 2**	**Step 3**	**Step 4**
Line up the decimal points.	Write the decimal point for the difference.	Regroup ones. Subtract tenths.	Subtract ones.
$\begin{array}{r} 9.2 \\ -\ 0.7 \\ \hline \end{array}$	$\begin{array}{r} 9.2 \\ -\ 0.7 \\ \hline . \end{array}$	$\begin{array}{r} {}^{8\,12} \\ 9\!\!.\!\!\cancel{2} \\ -\ 0.7 \\ \hline .5 \end{array}$	$\begin{array}{r} {}^{8\,12} \\ 9\!\!.\!\!\cancel{2} \\ -\ 0.7 \\ \hline 8.5 \end{array}$

> **TIP** When lining up decimals, add zero as a placeholder, if necessary.
>
> Add 5.16 + 8.7 + 4.02
>
> $\begin{array}{r} 5.16 \\ 8.7\mathbf{0} \\ +\ 4.02 \\ \hline 17.88 \end{array}$

Multiplying and Dividing Whole Numbers and Decimals

Factor × Factor = Product | Dividend ÷ Divisor = Quotient and (R) Remainder

$$\begin{array}{r} \text{Factor} \\ \times \ \text{Factor} \\ \hline \text{Product} \end{array}$$

$$\dfrac{\text{Quotient (R) Remainder}}{\text{Divisor}) \overline{\text{Dividend}}}$$

Skill 1 **Multiplying whole numbers**

Step 1

Multiply ones. Regroup.

$$\begin{array}{r} \overset{6}{4}07 \\ \times \quad 9 \\ \hline 3 \end{array}$$

Step 2

Multiply tens. Then add 6 tens.

THINK: 0 tens + 6 tens = 6 tens

$$\begin{array}{r} \overset{6}{4}07 \\ \times \quad 9 \\ \hline 63 \end{array}$$

Step 3

Multiply hundreds.

$$\begin{array}{r} \overset{6}{4}07 \\ \times \quad 9 \\ \hline 3{,}663 \end{array}$$

Skill 2 **Multiplying whole numbers and decimals**

Step 1

Multiply as you would whole numbers.

$$\begin{array}{r} 1.73 \\ \times \quad 8 \\ \hline 1384 \end{array}$$

Step 2

Count the number of decimal places in the factors. There are that many decimal places in the product.

$$\begin{array}{r} 1.73 \quad \text{2 decimal places} \\ \times \quad 8 \quad \text{0 decimal places} \\ \hline 13.84 \quad \text{2 decimal places} \end{array}$$

Skill 3 **Dividing decimals by whole numbers**

Step 1 Place the decimal point in the quotient directly above the decimal point in the dividend.

Step 2 Divide as you would whole numbers. Write additional zeros in the dividend as needed.

$$\begin{array}{r} 3.05 \\ 6)\overline{18.30} \\ \underline{18} \\ 3 \\ 0 \\ \underline{30} \\ 30 \\ \underline{30} \\ 0 \end{array}$$

TIP **Rounding the quotient:**

Rounding to the hundredths $0.485 \approx 0.49$
Rounding to the tenths $0.485 \approx 0.5$
Remember: $\approx$ means approximately equal to.

11

Practice

Add, subtract, multiply, or divide.

1.   2.5
     + 29.63

2.   802
        311
      + 89

3.   13.2
         14.57
       + 0.7

4.   964
       − 87

5.   69.5
        − 34.28

6.   85.21
        − 32.3

7.   609
       ×   5

8.   4.32
        ×   2

9.   7.07
        ×   4

10. $2\overline{)37}$

11. $7\overline{)6.3}$

12. $5\overline{)0.52}$

13. 4,892 + 3,605 = _____

14. 2,053 + 87 + 763 = _____

15. 9.6 + 13.05 + 10 = _____

16. 937 − 425 = _____

17. 58.32 − 29.54 = _____

18. 90.08 − 69.79 = _____

19. 3 × 221 = _____

20. 8 × 0.65 = _____

21. 4 × 0.09 = _____

22. 83 ÷ 4 = _____

23. 6,790 ÷ 9 = _____

24. 12.34 ÷ 4 = _____

Divide and round to the nearest tenth.

25. 9.92 ÷ 4 = _____

26. 5.48 ÷ 8 = _____

Divide and round to the nearest hundredth.

27. 8.59 ÷ 4 = _____

28. 6.87 ÷ 7 = _____

12

Name _____ Date _____

Solve.

29. It is 789 miles from Houston, Texas, to Atlanta, Georgia, and 2,496 miles from Atlanta to San Francisco, California. How many miles is it total from Houston to Atlanta and then on to San Francisco? _____

30. Ron spent $28.36 at the sports store and $16.09 at the deli. How much did he spend all together? _____

31. It is 2,078 miles from Dallas, Texas, to Seattle, Washington. You have already traveled 1,693 miles. How many more miles do you need to travel? _____

32. You need to buy some school supplies. The total cost of the supplies is $9.06. You have $7.98. How much more money do you need? _____

33. It is 379 miles from Los Angeles to San Francisco. You made this trip 7 times. How many miles did you travel in all? _____

34. Your class is selling school shirts for $15.75 each. The class sold 8 shirts during the first hour of the sale. How much money was collected during that hour? _____

35. An 8-oz box of chocolates costs $9.60. How much is the cost per ounce? _____

36. It is about 2,628 miles from Los Angeles to Washington, D.C. You made the trip in 6 days, traveling the same distance each day. How many miles did you travel each day? _____

Fractions, Decimals, and Percents

| Skill 1 | Renaming decimals as percents |

Rename 0.9 as a percent.

| Step 1 | Multiply by 100 by moving the decimal point 2 places to the right. Write additional zeros if necessary. | $0.90 \longrightarrow 90.0$ |
| Step 2 | Write the percent sign. | 90% |

Other examples

$0.89 \longrightarrow 0.89 \longrightarrow 89\%$ $0.034 \longrightarrow 0.034 \longrightarrow 3.4\%$ $8.4 \longrightarrow 8.40 \longrightarrow 840\%$

| Skill 2 | Renaming fractions as percents |

Rename $\frac{1}{5}$ as a percent.

| Step 1 | Write the fraction as a decimal. Divide the numerator by the denominator. Write additional zeros if necessary. | $\frac{1}{5} \longrightarrow 5\overline{)1.0}^{\,0.2}$ |
| Step 2 | Write the decimal as a percent. | $0.20 \longrightarrow 20\%$ |

| Skill 3 | Renaming percents as decimals |

Rename 3% as a decimal.

| Step 1 | Divide by 100 by moving the decimal point 2 places to the left. Write additional zeros if necessary. | $3\% \longrightarrow 0.03\%$ |
| Step 2 | Remove the percent sign. | 0.03 |

Other examples

$43\% \longrightarrow 0.43\% \longrightarrow 0.43$ $5.7\% \longrightarrow 0.05.7\% \longrightarrow 0.057$ $287\% \longrightarrow 2.87\% \longrightarrow 2.87$

Skill 4 — Renaming percents as fractions

Rename 80% as a fraction.

Step 1 Write the percent as a fraction with a denominator of 100.

$$80\% = \frac{80}{100}$$

Step 2 Write the fraction in lowest terms.

$$\frac{80}{100} = \frac{80 \div 20}{100 \div 20} = \frac{4}{5}$$

Other examples

$$75\% = \frac{75}{100} = \frac{75 \div 25}{100 \div 25} = \frac{3}{4}$$

$$150\% = \frac{150}{100} = \frac{150 \div 50}{100 \div 50} = \frac{3}{2} = 1\frac{1}{2}$$

Skill 5 — Expressing percents as decimals

Any percent can be expressed as a decimal.

Find 40% of 19.

Step 1 Write the problem as a number sentence.

40% of 19 is _____ ⟶ 40% × 19 = _____

Step 2 Rename the percent as a decimal.
THINK: 40% = 0.40 = 0.4

0.4 × 19 = _____

Step 3 Solve.

0.4 × 19 = 7.6

Skill 6 — Expressing percents as fractions

Sometimes it is easier to express a percent as a fraction.

Find 75% of 16.

Step 1 Write the problem as a number sentence.

75% of 16 is _____ ⟶ 75% × 16 = _____

Step 2 Rename the percent as a fraction.
THINK: $75\% = \frac{3}{4}$

$$\frac{3}{4} \times 16 = \underline{\hspace{1cm}}$$

Step 3 Solve.
THINK: $\frac{1}{4} \times 16 \longrightarrow 16 \div 4 = 4$
$\frac{3}{4} \times 16 \longrightarrow 3 \times 4 = 12$

$$\frac{3}{4} \times 16 = 12$$

So 75% of 16 is 12.

15

Practice

Rename as a percent.

1. $\frac{23}{100} =$ _____

2. $\frac{7}{100} =$ _____

3. $\frac{186}{100} =$ _____

4. $0.63 =$ _____

5. $0.058 =$ _____

6. $9 =$ _____

Rename as a decimal and as a percent.

7. $\frac{1}{4} =$ _____ $=$ _____

8. $\frac{7}{8} =$ _____ $=$ _____

9. $\frac{2}{5} =$ _____ $=$ _____

10. $3\frac{1}{2} =$ _____ $=$ _____

11. $9\frac{1}{8} =$ _____ $=$ _____

12. $5\frac{3}{5} =$ _____ $=$ _____

Rename as a decimal.

13. $24\% =$ _____

14. $18\% =$ _____

15. $2\% =$ _____

16. $2.8\% =$ _____

17. $0.05\% =$ _____

18. $438\% =$ _____

Rename as a fraction. Write fractions in lowest terms.

19. $70\% =$ _____

20. $40\% =$ _____

21. $85\% =$ _____

22. $110\% =$ _____

23. $187\% =$ _____

24. $204\% =$ _____

Find the answer. Decide whether to express the percent as a decimal or as a fraction.

25. 10% of $40 =$ _____

26. 25% of $24 =$ _____

27. 80% of $50 =$ _____

28. 40% of $15 =$ _____

29. 75% of $56 =$ _____

30. $33\frac{1}{3}\%$ of $36 =$ _____

31. $87\frac{1}{2}\%$ of $72 =$ _____

32. 50% of $73 =$ _____

33. $16\frac{2}{3}\%$ of $36 =$ _____

34. $37\frac{1}{2}\%$ of $64 =$ _____

35. 2% of $95 =$ _____

36. $33\frac{1}{3}\%$ of $39 =$ _____

16

Name _____ Date _____

Solve.

37. The trip between 2 towns is exactly 90 miles. You have gone 40% of this distance. How far have you gone? _____

38. Rosa received a grade of 88% on her vocabulary test. There were 25 fill-in-the-blank questions on the test. How many questions did Rosa get correct? _____

39. It takes Cara 35 minutes to walk to school. It takes Sue 80% of Cara's time. How long does it take Sue? _____

40. A sports watch originally cost $144. It is now being sold for 85% of its original price. How much does the watch cost now? _____

41. A wetsuit originally cost $750. It is now being sold at 30% off. How much has been deducted from the original cost of the wetsuit? _____

42. After a taste test, 40% of the 30 people interviewed preferred a new energy drink over orange juice. The rest preferred orange juice.

a. How many people preferred the energy drink? _____

b. How many people preferred orange juice? _____

Name _____   Date _____

Problem Solving Strategy:
Interpreting Data from Tables and Graphs

Situation:

The sales staff at Donney Motors keeps records of their car and truck sales. Contests are sometimes held to encourage special efforts to sell various cars and trucks. How can these records be used to identify a salesperson's performance?

Strategy:

You can use information in a **table** or a **bar graph** to solve a problem.

Applying the Strategy:

A. The salesperson who sold the greatest number of trucks in October won a flat-screen T.V. Who was it?

THINK: Look at the column labeled "Number of Trucks Sold."

| Step 1 | Which number is the greatest? (22) |

| Step 2 | Which name is on the same line as 22? (Ruth) |

Ruth sold the greatest number of trucks in October and won the TV.

October Sales	
Salesperson	**Number of Trucks Sold**
Ruth	22
Art	15
John	9
Eric	12
Mindy	4

B. Eric sold the greatest number of cars and trucks last year and won a free trip. How many cars and trucks did he sell?

THINK: Look at the bar above Eric's name.

| Step 1 | Between which 2 numbers does the bar lie? (250 and 300.) |

| Step 2 | Is the bar nearer to 250 or 300? (It is halfway between 250 and 300.) |

| Step 3 | What number is halfway between 250 and 300? (250 + 300 = 550) (550 ÷ 2 = 275) |

Eric sold 275 cars and trucks last year.

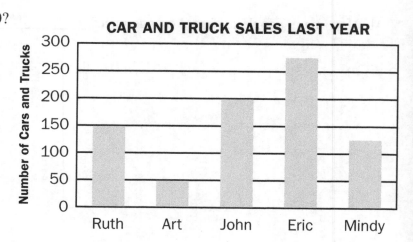

CAR AND TRUCK SALES LAST YEAR

Name _____   Date _____

Practice

Use the table of December sales for problems 1–2.

1. How many cars did Eric sell? _____

2. How many more cars did Mindy sell
   than Ruth? _____

December Sales	
Salesperson	**Number of Cars Sold**
Ruth	15
Art	25
John	20
Ginger	25
Eric	15
Mindy	20

The sales staff posted a bar graph to show the numbers of cars and trucks Donney Motors leased last year. Use the bar graph to answer problems 3–4.

3. How many crossovers were
   leased? _____

4. How many more 4-door
   sedans were leased than
   2-door sedans?

   _____

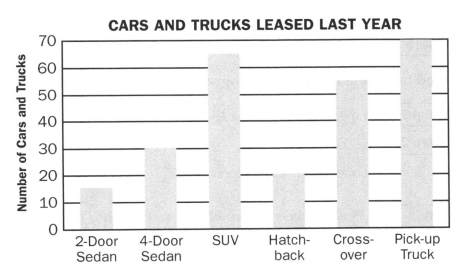

CARS AND TRUCKS LEASED LAST YEAR

5. Use the information in the "December Sales" table at the top of the page to construct a bar graph.
   Use this vertical scale: 0, 5, 10, 15, 20, 25, 30, 35.

The Mathematics of Trades and Professions, SV 9780547625560

Mean, Median, and Mode

> **Mean (average)**—The sum of a group of numbers divided by number of addends.
> **Median**—The middle number when a group of numbers is arranged in order from least to greatest.
> **Mode**—The number that occurs most frequently in a group of numbers.

Skill 1   **Finding the mean**

Find the mean of these basketball players' scores: 48, 36, 51, 72, 58.

| **Step 1** | Add the scores. | $48 + 36 + 51 + 72 + 58 = 265$ |
| **Step 2** | Divide by the number of scores. | $265 \div 5 = 53$ |

The mean, or average, of these scores is 53.

Skill 2   **Finding the median of an odd number of scores**

Find the median of these bowling scores: 126, 108, 145, 108, 117.

| **Step 1** | Arrange the scores in order. | 108   108   117   126   145 |
| **Step 2** | Find the middle score. | 117 |

The median of these scores is 117.

Skill 3   **Finding the median of an even number of scores**

Find the median of these bowling scores: 139, 106, 145, 113, 128, 109.

Step 1	Arrange the scores in order.	106 109 113 128 139 145
Step 2	Find the middle score. (**THINK:** There is no *one* middle number.)	113 128
Step 3	Find the mean of the two middle scores.	$113 + 128 = 241 \div 2 = 120.5$

The median of these scores is 120.5.

Skill 4   **Finding the mode**

Find the mode of these race times: 9.3, 9.6, 9.2, 10.2, 9.6, 10.1, 9.5.

Find the time that occurs most often.   9.6 occurs twice.

The mode of these scores is 9.6.

Name _____   Date _____

Practice

Find the mean.

1. 86, 90, 94 _____

2. 4.2, 8.5, 2.6 _____

3. 172, 550, 293, 413 _____

4. 95, 63, 12, 102 _____

5. 20, 18, 6, 10, 16 _____

6. 0.18, 0.45, 0.34, 0.51, 0.27 _____

Find the median.

7. 7, 13, 25, 46, 8 _____

8. 9, 12, 7, 24, 18 _____

9. 1.3, 6.2, 8.9, 2.4, 5.6 _____

10. 1.3, 5.2, 4.7, 1.6, 4.1, 7.3 _____

Find the mode.

11. 1, 3, 5, 9, 3, 6, 7, 8 _____

12. 9.6, 4.5, 1.8, 4.7, 6.7, 1.8, 3.2 _____

Find the mean, the median, and the mode. Round the mean and median to the nearest tenth.

13. 56, 78, 92   mean _____   median _____   mode _____

14. 6.3, 2.5, 10.1   mean _____   median _____   mode _____

15. 302, 220, 220, 208   mean _____   median _____   mode _____

16. 75, 93, 89, 75, 84   mean _____   median _____   mode _____

17. 6.1, 5.9, 4.2, 5.9, 10.7   mean _____   median _____   mode _____

Solve.

18. Six judges scored a diving contest. On one dive, 2 judges gave a 7.5. The other scores were 8.0, 7.9, 6.8, and 7.3. What are the mean, median, and mode of these scores?

    mean _____   median _____   mode _____

Extension   **Using a Tally**

Each time Ed played miniature golf, he made a tally mark next to his score.

1. How many games did Ed play? _____
2. What are his two mode scores? _____
3. What is his median score? _____
4. What is the total of the scores of:
   (a) 69? _____; (b) 68? _____; (c) 67? _____
5. What is his mean score rounded to the nearest hundredth? _____

Score	Total	Score	Total
72 - ̶I̶I̶I̶I̶ I	360	69 - ̶I̶I̶I̶I̶ II	
71 - ̶I̶I̶I̶I̶ III	568	68 - III	
70 - ̶I̶I̶I̶I̶ III	560	67 - II	

Basic Operations on a Calculator

When you want to compute quickly and accurately with greater numbers, you can use a calculator.

The four basic operations (addition, subtraction, multiplication, and division) can be performed easily.

Operation	Calculator Entry	Calculator Display
Add: 49,567 + 78,078	4 9 5 6 7 + 7 8 0 7 8 =	127.645
Subtract: 34.014 − 5.708	3 4 . 0 1 4 − 5 . 7 0 8 =	28.306
Multiply: 908 × 0.045	9 0 8 × 0 . 0 4 5 =	40.86
Divide: 4.9452 ÷ 0.078	4 . 9 4 5 2 ÷ 0 . 0 7 8 =	63.4

You can use a calculator to do a series of operations without using the [=] **key (is equal to)** after each operation.

Find 45.09 − 6 + 4.7 − 18.

Calculator Entry	Calculator Display
4 5 . 0 9 − 6 +	39.09
4 . 7 −	43.79
1 8 =	25.79

So, 45.09 − 6 + 4.7 − 18 = 25.79.

> **TIP** The [CE] key (Clear Entry) can help you when you have entered a wrong number into the calculator.

Name _____ Date _____

Think About It

1. For which operations will the order in which you enter two numbers not affect the answer? Why?

_____

2. The entry below was made on two different calculators. One calculator displayed the answer 6.15. The other calculator displayed the answer 16.4. Explain the different answers.

[4][.][5][×][3][+][7][−][8][.][2][÷][2][=]

_____

_____

Practice

Use a calculator to compute.

1. 1,294,588 − 346,183 = _____

2. 5,496 + 2,659 = _____

3. 27,587 ÷ 49 = _____

4. 735.8 − 35.635 = _____

5. 425.36 × 18.3 = _____

6. 46.84 × 7.03 ÷ 2 = _____

7. 36.5 divided into 65,700 = _____

8. 0.4 divided into 0.028 = _____

Divide and round to the nearest tenth.

9. $18.2\overline{)375}$

10. $3.79\overline{)463}$

Divide and round to the nearest hundredth.

11. 0.37 ÷ 2.9 = _____

12. $53.8\overline{)2.847}$

Compute from left to right.

13. 933.6 − 3.498 + 364.9 − 483.78 = _____

14. 28.64 ÷ 0.2 × 0.45 ÷ 15 = _____

Solve.

15. Joe's car odometer read 27,314 miles when he left for summer vacation. Three months later, the odometer read 35,278 miles. How far had Joe traveled? _____

16. Gary ordered 500 sheets of paper. When they arrived, they formed a pile 4.5 centimeters high. How thick was each sheet? _____

Computing Mentally

You may often find it easier to compute mentally than to use a pencil and paper or even a calculator. You can add mentally by using numbers that are **multiples of 10** and then adjusting.

Example 1: You are buying a shirt for $19 and a jacket for $44. Mentally compute the cost of the shirt and the jacket.

Add: $19 + $44
THINK: $19 is $1 less than $20. $20 + $44 = $64

So $19 + $44 is $1 less than $64, or $63.

The shirt and the jacket will cost $63.

You can subtract mentally in the same way.

Example 2: Subtract:
 a. 94 − 18
  THINK: 18 is 2 less than 20.

  94 − 20 = 74
  So 94 − 18 is 2 more than 74, or 76.

 b. 465 − 190
  THINK: 190 is 10 less than 200.

  465 − 200 = 265
  So 465 − 190 is 10 more than 265, or 275.

Mental computation is also commonly used when you multiply or divide by **powers of 10**, such as 10, 100, or 1,000.

Example 3: Multiply: 100×87.30
THINK: The product must be greater than 87.30, so move the decimal point to the right.

  $100 \times 87.30 = 8,730$
  2 zeros
    2 places right

Example 4: Divide: $38,430 \div 1,000$
THINK: The quotient must be less than 38,430, so move the decimal point to the left.

  $38,430 \div 1,000 = 38.43$
  3 places left
    3 zeros

Name _____ Date _____

1. Ricky argues that mental computation is a waste of time, since he has a calculator. How would you convince Ricky that he is wrong?

_____

_____

Practice

Use mental computation to add or subtract.

1. 46 + 19 = _____

2. 25 + 48 = _____

3. 467 + 310 = _____

4. 36¢ + 29¢ = _____

5. $6.55 + $3.39 = _____

6. 6.57 + 2.99 = _____

7. 47 − 19 = _____

8. 376 − 102 = _____

9. 50¢ − 14¢ = _____

10. $875 − $280 = _____

11. $1.70 − $0.61 = _____

12. 7.80 − 4.38 = _____

Use mental computation to multiply or divide.

13. 100 × 6.8 = _____

14. 10 × 0.532 = _____

15. 100 × 759.5 = _____

16. 19.4 ÷ 10 = _____

17. 28.5 ÷ 100 = _____

18. 2,045 ÷ 100 = _____

Solve using mental computation.

19. A $550 dishwasher is marked down by $59. How much does the dishwasher now sell for?

_____

20. The 100 members of a marching band agree to split the $7,340.00 cost of their trip. What is each member's share? _____

Extension **Multiplying mentally by 50 and by 25.**

Multiply: 50 × 2.8
THINK: 100 × 2.8 = 280
Since 50 = 100 ÷ 2, then 50 × 2.8 = 280 ÷ 2 = 140.

Multiply: 25 × 16.4
THINK: 100 × 16.4 = 1,640
Since 25 = 100 ÷ 4, then 25 × 16.4 = 1,640 ÷ 4 = 410.

Use mental computation to multiply.

1. 50 × 84 = _____

2. 25 × 240 = _____

3. 50 × 120 = _____

Name _____   Date _____

Estimating Sums and Differences

A common way to **estimate** sums is to round each number to the same **place value** and then add mentally.

Example 1: Estimate the total population of the four towns in Fairview County.

Town	Greenfield	Salem	Goshen	Wells
Population	21,284	3,487	38,372	10,480

| Step 1 | Round each number to the thousands place. |

$$
\begin{array}{rcr}
21,284 & \longrightarrow & 21,000 \\
3,487 & \longrightarrow & 3,000 \\
38,372 & \longrightarrow & 38,000 \\
+\ 10,480 & \longrightarrow & +\ 10,000 \\
\hline
 & & 72,000
\end{array}
$$

| Step 2 | Add. |

72,000 is a good estimate for the total population.

Example 2:

a. Estimate: 31.07 + 0.56 + 3.87

| Step 1 | Round each number to the tenths place. |

$$
\begin{array}{rcr}
31.07 & \longrightarrow & 31.1 \\
0.56 & \longrightarrow & 0.6 \\
+\ 3.87 & \longrightarrow & +\ 3.9 \\
\hline
 & & 35.6
\end{array}
$$

| Step 2 | Add. |

b. Estimate: 95¢ + $2.09 + $5.75

| Step 1 | Round each number to the ones place. |

$$
\begin{array}{rcr}
\$0.95 & \longrightarrow & \$1 \\
\$2.09 & \longrightarrow & \$2 \\
+\ \$5.75 & \longrightarrow & +\ \$6 \\
\hline
 & & \$9
\end{array}
$$

| Step 2 | Add. |

The same estimating rules are used for subtraction.

Example 3:

a. Estimate: 27,387 − 2,163

| Step 1 | Round each number to the thousands place. |

$$
\begin{array}{rcr}
27,387 & \longrightarrow & 27,000 \\
-\ 2,163 & \longrightarrow & -\ 2,000 \\
\hline
 & & 25,000
\end{array}
$$

| Step 2 | Subtract. |

b. Estimate: 0.37 − 0.097

| Step 1 | Round each number to the tenths place. |

$$
\begin{array}{rcr}
0.37 & \longrightarrow & 0.4 \\
-\ 0.097 & \longrightarrow & -\ 0.1 \\
\hline
 & & 0.3
\end{array}
$$

| Step 2 | Subtract. |

Name _____ Date _____

1. How is mental computation different from estimation?

_____

_____

2. To estimate $4.80 + $2.25 + $3.40, Gail rounded up and down and used $5 + $2 + $3 = $10. Gail's mother rounded up and used $5 + $3 + $4 = $12. What are some advantages of doing estimation the second way?

_____

_____

Practice

Estimate the sum or difference by rounding to the place value indicated.

1.   378 (hundreds)
    + 128

2.   572 (tens)
    628
    + 84

3. $6.84 (ones)
    + $3.14

4. $2.18 (ones)
    $0.95
    + $1.32

5.   893.5 (tens)
    + 37.75

6.   0.099 (tenths)
    + 0.43

7.   47,564 (thousands)
    + 6,891

8.   0.028 (hundredths)
    + 0.0095

9.   432 (tens)
    − 19

10. 88,271 (ten thousands)
    − 27,557

11. $0.82 (tenths)
    − $0.17

12. $13.72 (ones)
    − $0.84

13. 248.2 (tens)
    − 24.9

14. 4.89 (ones)
    − 0.75

15. $795.77 (ones)
    − $9.56

Solve.

16. Ben bought a snack for $3.08. About how much change did he get from $5.00? _____

17. A television is advertised at Bob's Appliances for $379. The same television is on sale at Acme Audio for $285. About how much can be saved by buying it at Acme? _____

Estimating Products and Quotients

A common way to estimate products and quotients is to round each number to its **greatest place** and then compute mentally.

Example 1: There were 285 wildlife pamphlets left to be distributed. Six friends shared the task. About how many pamphlets must each person hand out if they share the job?

| **Step 1** | Round. | 285 rounds to 300. Since 6 is a 1-digit number, it does not need to be rounded. |

| **Step 2** | Divide. | 300 ÷ 6 = 50. |

So each person will hand out about 50 pamphlets.

Example 2:
   a. Estimate: 2,789 × 48

| **Step 1** | Round. | 3,000 × 50 |

| **Step 2** | Multiply. | 150,000 |

   b. Estimate: 22,270 ÷ 39

| **Step 1** | Round. | 20,000 ÷ 40 |

| **Step 2** | Divide. | 500 |

When multiplying or dividing decimals or money amounts, estimate by rounding each number to its **greatest nonzero place**.

Example 3:
   a. Estimate: 78 × $0.29

| **Step 1** | Round. | 80 × $0.30 |

| **Step 2** | Multiply. | $24 |

   b. Estimate: 324.8 ÷ 4.87

| **Step 1** | Round. | 300 ÷ 5 |

| **Step 2** | Divide. | 60 |

Name _____ Date _____

1. Laura calculated that 3.2×16.8 is 5.376. Estimate and explain why Laura's answer cannot be correct.

_____

_____

_____

Practice

Estimate the product and quotient.

1. $4{,}812 \times 44 \approx$ _____

2. $52 \times \$12.75 \approx$ _____

3. $360 \times \$19.95 \approx$ _____

4. $82 \times 5.8 \approx$ _____

5. $8.9 \times 3.13 \approx$ _____

6. $27.19 \times 8.47 \approx$ _____

7. $385 \times \$0.82 \approx$ _____

8. $185 \times 0.89 \approx$ _____

9. $0.65 \times 0.34 \approx$ _____

10. $216 \div 39 \approx$ _____

11. $875 \div 182 \approx$ _____

12. $\$11.80 \div 5 \approx$ _____

13. $\$43.60 \div 22 \approx$ _____

14. $\$293 \div 53 \approx$ _____

15. $87 \div 2.87 \approx$ _____

16. $957.5 \div 46 \approx$ _____

17. $35.7 \div 5.4 \approx$ _____

18. $962.1 \div 19.3 \approx$ _____

Use the menu for problems 19–20.

19. About how much will 5 juices cost? _____

20. About how many hamburgers can be bought for $18.00? _____

MENU	
Hamburgers	**$2.89**
Hot Dogs	**$2.15**
Chicken Sandwich	**$3.49**
Salad	**$2.50**
Juice	**$1.19**
Apple Slices	**$0.79**
Popcorn	**$0.75**

Solve.

21. CDs cost $9.75 each. About how much will 12 CDs cost? _____

22. Women's dresses cost $219.50 each. About how many dresses can be bought for $900.00? _____

Name _____ Date _____

Problem Solving Strategy: Which Way to Compute?

Situation:

Suppose you are asked to find the cost of 5 pairs of socks at $1.95 a pair plus a sales tax of $0.40. Which way would you use to compute the answer?

Strategy:

Use paper and pencil skills, a calculator, or mental computation skills depending on the situation, the numbers involved, or your own personal preference.

Applying the Strategy:

Joan took out a pencil and computed:

$$\begin{array}{r} \$1.95 \\ \times \quad 5 \\ \hline \$9.75 \\ + \ 0.40 \\ \hline \$10.15 \end{array}$$

Jill took out a calculator and computed:

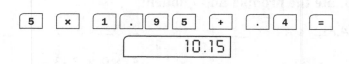

Jackie thought:

$1.95 is 5¢ less than $2. So 5 pairs are 25¢ less than $10, or $9.75, plus 40¢.

40¢ is 25¢ plus 15¢. So $9.75 plus 25¢ is $10, plus 15¢ is $10.15.

Notice that Joan, Jill, and Jackie all got the same answer.

Other Situations:

A. What is the best way to compute the amount of change that Ray received if he paid $5.00 for a $2.97 meal?

Ray can easily compute this mentally.
He thinks: $2.97 is 3¢ less than $3.00.
$5.00 − $3.00 is $2.00.

So $5.00 − $2.97 is $2.00 plus 3¢, or $2.03.

B. What is the best way for Alvin to compute the new balance in the class treasury? The balance was $357.82. He made a deposit of $182.14 and then made a withdrawal of $78.50.

Alvin needs an exact answer, and the numbers are too great to use mental computation. So he uses his calculator or paper and pencil to get $461.46.

C. What is the best way for Mr. Lee to compute the total length of pipe if one piece is $4\frac{3}{4}$ feet long, and the other is $2\frac{7}{8}$ feet long?

If Mr. Lee wants an exact answer, it is unlikely that he will use mental computation or convert to decimals and use a calculator. He will probably use paper and pencil.

$$\begin{array}{r} 4\frac{3}{4} \ = \ 4\frac{6}{8} \\ + \ 2\frac{7}{8} \ = \ + \ 2\frac{7}{8} \\ \hline 6\frac{13}{8} = 7\frac{5}{8} \text{ feet} \end{array}$$

Name _____ Date _____

1. Show how Alvin could have solved his problem with paper and pencil instead of a calculator. Discuss which method you prefer and why.

_____

_____

_____

_____

2. Show how Mr. Lee could have solved his problem using a calculator. Discuss why using a calculator to find the answer gives a different answer from what Mr. Lee found.

_____

_____

_____

_____

Practice

Identify whether you would most likely use paper and pencil, a calculator, or mental computation to compute.

1. Find the tip for a server. _____

2. Find the walking time to school. _____

3. Find the cost of 17 items in the grocery store. _____

4. Find the average weight of the students in your class. _____

Use two different methods to compute. Identify the most efficient method.

5. Find the actual distance between two cities that are $2\frac{1}{4}$ inches apart on a map with a scale of 1 inch per 40 miles.

6. Find the cost per person if 27 people spent a total of $200.

Part I Review

Vocabulary

Choose the letter of the word(s) that completes the sentence.

1. You can compute mentally by using numbers that are _____ of ten.

   a. factors   **b.** multiples   **c.** remainders

2. The number that occurs most frequently in a group of numbers is called the _____.

   a. mean   **b.** median   **c.** mode

3. You can estimate with whole numbers and decimals by rounding each number to its _____.

   a. last place   **b.** greatest nonzero place   **c.** least nonzero place

Skills

Add, subtract, multiply, or divide.

4. $8{,}666 + 530 + 741 =$ _____   **5.** $2.8 + 19.17 + 10.03 =$ _____   **6.** $741 + 2{,}037 + 667 =$ _____

7. $90{,}468 - 37{,}491 =$ _____   **8.** $84.3 - 55.76 =$ _____   **9.** $11.07 - 9.21 =$ _____

10. $2 \times 43 =$ _____   **11.** $7 \times 209 =$ _____   **12.** $5 \times 3.23 =$ _____

13. $6{,}072 \div 8 =$ _____   **14.** $468 \div 2 =$ _____   **15.** $0.6 \div 4 =$ _____

Rename as a percent.

16. $\dfrac{6}{100}$ _____   **17.** $\dfrac{400}{100}$ _____   **18.** $\dfrac{275}{100}$ _____

19. 0.48 _____   **20.** 0.09 _____   **21.** 0.035 _____

Rename as a decimal.

22. 43% _____   **23.** 3.6% _____   **24.** 600% _____

Find the answer.

25. 40% of 25 _____   **26.** $12\frac{1}{2}\%$ of 48 _____   **27.** 60% of 200 _____

Use a calculator to compute.

28. $4,689 + 8,873 + 472 =$ _____

29. $58.93 \times 39.58 =$ _____

30. $7 + 39.88 - 15.938 =$ _____

31. $20.5 \times 51.22 \div 16.4 =$ _____

Compute mentally.

32. $357 + 298 =$ _____

33. $10 \times 8.9 =$ _____

34. $866 \div 100 =$ _____

35. $74,803 \div 1,000 =$ _____

Estimate.

36. $6,835 + 3,128 \approx$ _____

37. $13.89 - 4.935 \approx$ _____

38. $0.34 \times 0.17 \approx$ _____

39. $78 \div 4 \approx$ _____

40. $3\frac{2}{3} + 22\frac{1}{4} \approx$ _____

41. $9\frac{4}{5} - 1\frac{1}{3} \approx$ _____

Solve.

42. A traveling salesperson drove 653 miles in April. In May, she drove 1,008 miles, and in June, 398 miles. What was the total number of miles that the salesperson drove during these 3 months? _____

43. A textile manufacturer must finish filling an order for 3,020 yards of fabric. He has already shipped 1,950 yards. How many more yards must he ship? _____

44. Ben cut a $37\frac{3}{8}$-inch board from a board $50\frac{1}{2}$ inches long. About how much wood is left? _____

45. CDs are on sale for $6.79 each. Will $25 be enough to buy 4 CDs? _____

Name _____   Date _____

Part I Test

Add, subtract, multiply, or divide.

1. 8,732
    + 1,487

2.   5.6
    + 35.7

3. 16.7
    0.89
    + 3.65

4. 4,376
    − 2,923

5. 87.6
    − 29.83

6. 50.06
    − 17.39

7. 803
    ×   7

8.   5.9
    ×   8

9. 6.08
    ×   7

10. $3\overline{)2{,}464}$

11. $6\overline{)12.6}$

12. $9\overline{)4.68}$

Divide and round to the nearest hundredth.

13. $7\overline{)3.86}$

14. $5\overline{)9.13}$

15. $6\overline{)5.08}$

Rename as a percent.

16. 71 per 100 _____

17. 0.026 _____

18. $\frac{4}{5}$ _____

19. $1\frac{3}{5}$ _____

20. 2.793 _____

21. 25 of 50 _____

Rename as a decimal and as a fraction.

22. 3.6%   ⟶   decimal _____   ⟶   fraction _____

23. 60%   ⟶   decimal _____   ⟶   fraction _____

24. 250%   ⟶   decimal _____   ⟶   fraction _____

Use the following numbers to answer questions 25–27.

15, 12, 10, 15, 18

25. Find the mean: _____

26. Find the median: _____

27. Find the mode: _____

The Mathematics of Trades and Professions, SV 9780547625560

Name _____ Date _____

Use a calculator to compute.

28. $8{,}732 + 1{,}487 =$ _____

29. $16.7 + 0.89 + 3.65 =$ _____

30. $4{,}376 - 2{,}923 =$ _____

31. $50.06 - 17.39 =$ _____

32. $780.44 \div 8.72 =$ _____

33. $141.82 \times 15.6 \div 302.88 =$ _____

Use mental computation to add, subtract, multiply, or divide.

34. $453 + 210 =$ _____

35. $\$415 + \$390 =$ _____

36. $8.15 + 9.79 =$ _____

37. $31 - 19 =$ _____

38. $\$5.00 - \$2.98 =$ _____

39. $100 \times 23 =$ _____

40. $78.4 \div 10 =$ _____

41. $.0245 \times 1{,}000 =$ _____

42. $39.58 \div 10 =$ _____

Estimate.

43. $875 + 786 \approx$ _____

44. $714 - 298 \approx$ _____

45. $\$4.86 + \$8.52 \approx$ _____

46. $2.35 - 1.45 \approx$ _____

47. $62 \times 78 \approx$ _____

48. $62.8 \div 6.2 \approx$ _____

Estimate to choose the reasonable answer.

49. $86 + 74.9 + 365.4 \approx$ _____   **a.** 5.263   **b.** 526.3   **c.** 5,263

50. $5{,}860 \div 15 \approx$ _____   **a.** 3.907   **b.** 39.07   **c.** 390.7

Solve.

51. Jon's four coworkers took him out to lunch for his birthday. The total bill was $58. Jon's coworkers paid his portion. How much did each person's equal share cost? _____

52. Tomato sauce costs 89¢ per can, noodles cost $1.50 per package, grated cheese costs $1.85 per container, and baseball cards cost $2 per pack. If Kenny needs two cans of sauce, one package of noodles, and one container of cheese, how many packs of cards can Kenny buy if he has $10? _____

53. Sue is cutting pieces of ribbon $8\frac{1}{8}$ inches long. About how many pieces can she cut from a 6-foot length of ribbon? _____

   The Mathematics of Trades and Professions, SV 9780547625560

Part II:
Trade Industries

Pre-Skills Test

Multiply.

1. $145 \times \$50 =$ _____

2. $1{,}500 \times \$75 =$ _____

3. $180 \times 36¢ =$ _____

4. $225 \times 56¢ =$ _____

5. $20 \times 5\frac{1}{2} =$ _____

6. $8 \times 6\frac{2}{3} =$ _____

7. $150 \times 4\frac{2}{5} =$ _____

8. $80 \times 5\frac{3}{4} =$ _____

9. $2 \times \frac{2}{3} \times 16 =$ _____

10. $2 \times \frac{1}{3} \times 8 =$ _____

11. $4 \times \frac{1}{2} \times 14 =$ _____

12. $6 \times \frac{3}{8} \times 1\frac{1}{4} =$ _____

Estimate the quotient.

13. $3{,}326 \div 400 =$ _____

14. $1{,}807 \div 290 =$ _____

15. $2{,}680 \div 300 =$ _____

Divide and round to the nearest tenth.

16. $750 \div 9 =$ _____

17. $3{,}873 \div 15 =$ _____

18. $2{,}580 \div 27 =$ _____

Add or subtract.

19. $4\frac{1}{2} + \frac{3}{8} =$ _____

20. $\frac{5}{8} + 5\frac{3}{4} =$ _____

21. $3\frac{1}{3} - \frac{2}{3} =$ _____

Part II
The Mathematics of Trades and Professions, SV 9780547625560

Name _____   Date _____

Convert to feet.

22. 15 yd = _____

23. 20 yd = _____

24. 9 yd = _____

25. $5\frac{1}{3}$ yd = _____

26. 24 yd 2 ft = _____

27. 17 yd 8 ft = _____

Convert to yards.

28. 18 ft = _____

29. 288 ft = _____

30. 100 ft = _____

31. 85 ft = _____

32. 477 ft = _____

33. 1,350 ft = _____

Find the perimeter.

34. _____

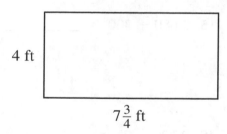

4 ft

$7\frac{3}{4}$ ft

35. _____

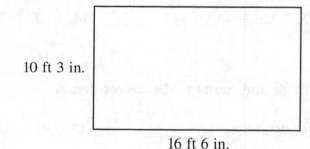

10 ft 3 in.

16 ft 6 in.

Find the area.

36. _____

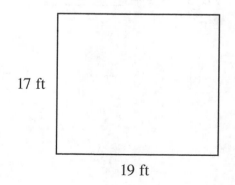

17 ft

19 ft

37. _____

10 ft 8 in.

22 ft 6 in.

Name _____ Date _____

Carpentry

Carpenters usually estimate the cost of a job on a square-foot basis. New residential construction is estimated at about $80 per square foot, and renovation work is estimated at about $100 per square foot.

Example 1: Charles Atamian is a carpenter who submits an estimate to build a 24 ft by 30 ft addition to a house. At $80 per square ft, how much does he estimate the job will cost?

| **Step 1** | Find the number of square ft (area).
24 ft × 30 ft = 720 square ft

| **Step 2** | Multiply to estimate the cost.
720 × $80 = $57,600

Charles estimates the addition will cost $57,600.

Carpenters usually buy lumber by the **board foot**. A board foot is the amount of wood in a board 1-in. thick by 1-ft wide by 1-ft long.

Example 2: How many board feet are in one 16-ft-long piece of 2 in. by 4 in. lumber?

THINK: Thickness: 2 in.   Width: 4 in.   Length: 16 ft

Since 4 in. = $\frac{1}{3}$ ft, the board is 2 in. by $\frac{1}{3}$ ft by 16 ft.

Multiply to find the board feet.   2 in. × $\frac{1}{3}$ ft × 16 ft = $\frac{(32)}{3}$ = $10\frac{2}{3}$

The board contains $10\frac{2}{3}$ board ft.

The Mathematics of Trades and Professions, SV 9780547625560

Example 3: Charles needs 36 16-ft-long 2 in. by 8 in. boards for the rafters and 60 8-ft-long 2 in. by 4 in. boards for the wall studs. At 36¢ per board ft, how much will the lumber cost?

Step 1 Find the number of board feet in each size of lumber.

$$2 \text{ in.} \times 8 \text{ in.} \times 16 \text{ ft} = 2 \text{ in.} \times \frac{2}{3} \text{ ft} \times 16 \text{ ft} = \frac{(64)}{3} = 21\frac{1}{3} \text{ board feet}$$

$$2 \text{ in.} \times 4 \text{ in.} \times 8 \text{ ft} = 2 \text{ in.} \times \frac{1}{3} \text{ ft} \times 8 \text{ ft} = \frac{(16)}{3} = 5\frac{1}{3} \text{ board feet}$$

Step 2 Multiply by the number of boards.

$$36 \text{ boards} \times 21\frac{1}{3} \text{ board ft} = 768 \text{ board ft}$$

$$60 \text{ boards} \times 5\frac{1}{3} \text{ board ft} = 320 \text{ board ft}$$

Step 3 Add.

$$
\begin{array}{r}
768 \text{ board feet} \\
+ \ 320 \text{ board feet} \\
\hline
\text{Total} \quad 1{,}088 \text{ board feet}
\end{array}
$$

Step 4 Multiply by the cost per board foot.

$$1{,}088 \text{ board ft} \times \$0.36 = \$391.68$$

The lumber will cost $391.68.

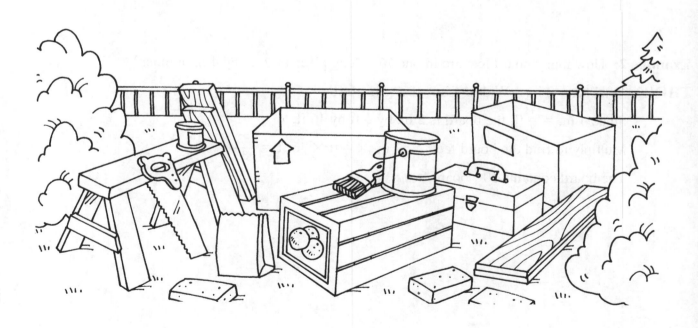

The Mathematics of Trades and Professions, SV 9780547625560

Name _____ Date _____

1. Why is the cost of renovation work often higher than the cost of new construction?

   _____

   _____

   _____

2. What is the difference between 1 board foot and 1 linear, or straight-measured, foot of lumber?

   _____

   _____

   _____

   _____

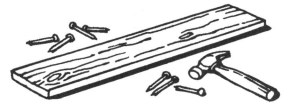

Practice

Remember to estimate whenever you use your calculator.

Find the estimated cost. Estimate new construction at $80 per square ft and renovation work at $100 per square ft.

1. New: 9 ft by 12 ft _____

2. New: 20 ft by 24 ft _____

3. New 28 ft by 40 ft _____

4. Renovation: 10 ft by 15 ft _____

5. Renovation: 18 ft by 30 ft _____

6. Renovation: 20 ft by 45 ft _____

7. New: 8 ft by 36 ft, and
   Renovation: 50 ft by 64 ft _____

8. New: 14 ft by 18 ft, and
   Renovation: 16 ft by 45 ft _____

9. New: 40 ft by 12 ft, and
   Renovation: 25 ft by 64 ft _____

Name _____ Date _____

Complete the table.

Board Size	Length of Board	Number of Boards	Number of Board Feet	Cost per Board Foot	Total Cost
1 in. by 6 in.	12 ft	2	10. _____	37.5¢	11. _____
2 in. by 4 in.	10 ft	24	12. _____	27¢	13. _____
2 in. by 6 in.	16 ft	15	14. _____	32.5¢	15. _____
1 in. by 10 in.	6 ft	8	16. _____	40¢	17. _____
2 in. by 8 in.	14 ft	30	18. _____	29.5¢	19. _____

Complete to find the total cost of the purchase.

Ray's Lumber Company			
Qty.	Item	Unit Cost	Total
10	2 in. by 6 in. by 12 ft board	30¢/board foot	20. _____
18	2 in. by 4 in. by 12 ft board	30¢/board foot	21. _____
6	4 ft by 8 ft plywood	$14.95/sheet	22. _____
4 pkg.	gray shingles	$19.75/pkg.	23. _____
5 lb	common nails	62¢/lb	24. _____
		Total	25. _____

The Mathematics of Trades and Professions, SV 9780547625560

Problem Solving Application: Carpenter

Kristin Leonard is a carpenter. In her work, she must be able to make careful measurements. Often, she needs to use fractions and mixed numbers.

A board 9 ft long is cut into sections of the given length. How many sections are there?

1. Sections $\frac{3}{4}$ ft long _____

2. Sections $1\frac{1}{2}$ ft long _____

3. Sections 27 in. long _____

A board $7\frac{1}{2}$ ft long is cut into equal parts. How long is each part?

4. 6 equal parts _____

5. 10 equal parts _____

6. 5 equal parts _____

Each drawing represents a board marked off into equal parts. Find the total length of the board.

7. _____

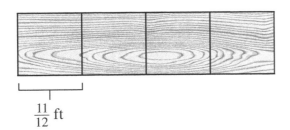

$\frac{11}{12}$ ft

8. _____

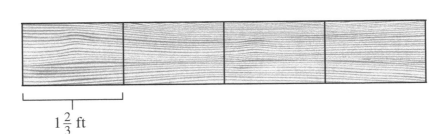

$1\frac{2}{3}$ ft

Write the measurement using a fraction or a mixed number in lowest terms.

9. 0.75 yd _____

10. 2.5 in. _____

11. 1.125 in. _____

12. 0.9375 in. _____

13. 6.667 ft _____

14. 2.875 ft _____

Solve.

15. A board of lumber called a "2-by-4" is actually $1\frac{5}{8}$ in. thick and $3\frac{5}{8}$ in. wide. Kristen stacks three boards as shown below. What is the total height of the stack? _____

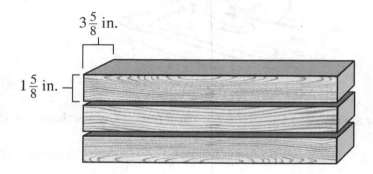

$3\frac{5}{8}$ in.

$1\frac{5}{8}$ in.

16. Kristen had a board $11\frac{1}{2}$ ft long. She sawed it in half and used one piece. Then she sawed the remaining piece in half and used one of the pieces. How long was the remaining piece?

_____

Electrical Contracting

Tom Williams is an **electrical contractor**. He wires houses and buildings to distribute the flow of electricity. Electricians estimate the materials they will need to complete a job.

Example 1: If Tom averages 75 ft of wire per room when wiring a new home, how many 100-ft coils of wire should be purchased for a 9-room house?

Step 1	Multiply to estimate the total amount of wire.

9×75 ft $= 675$ ft

Step 2	Divide to find the number of coils.

675 ft $\div$ 100 ft per coil $= 6.75$ coils
Round up to be sure there is enough.
$6.75 \approx 7$ coils

Tom should purchase 7 coils of wire.

Example 2: For an addition to a house, Tom ordered 200 ft of #14 electrical cable wire, 9 outlet boxes, 3 switches, and 6 3-prong receptacles. Find the total cost of the materials if the wire costs $39.50 per 100 ft, the outlet boxes are $4.95 each, the switches are $3.75 each, and the receptacles are $3.25 each.

Step 1	Multiply to find the total cost of each item.

200 ft of #14 electrical cable wire	at $39.50 per 100 ft	$2 \times \$39.50 =$	$79.00
9 outlet boxes	at $4.95 each	$9 \times \$4.95 =$	$44.55
3 switches	at $3.75 each	$3 \times \$3.75 =$	$11.25
6 3-prong receptacles	at $3.25 each	$6 \times \$3.25 =$	$19.50

Step 2	Add to find the total cost.

$79.00 + $44.55 + $11.25 + $19.50 = $154.30

The materials will cost about $154.30.

Example 3: For most jobs, Tom charges $24.75 per hour for labor for himself and $15.45 per hour for his assistant. What is the labor charge for a job on which they work together for $7\frac{1}{2}$ hours?

Step 1	Multiply to find the total charges.

electrician   7.5 hours × $24.75/hour = $185.625 ≈ $185.63

assistant   7.5 hours × $15.45/hour = $115.875 ≈ $115.88

Step 2	Add to find the total.

$185.63 + $115.88 = $301.51

The total labor charge is $301.51.

Think About It

1. Why do most building codes require that electrical work be done by licensed electricians?

_____

_____

_____

2. What purpose do the fuses and circuit breakers play in a building's electrical system?

_____

_____

_____

Practice

Remember to estimate whenever you use your calculator.

Complete the table.

Average Number of Feet of Wire per Room	Number of Rooms	Number of 100-ft Coils Needed	Cost per 100 ft	Total Cost
75	3	**1.** _____	$29.95	**2.** _____
65	5	**3.** _____	$32.50	**4.** _____
90	6	**5.** _____	$39.65	**6.** _____
120	8	**7.** _____	$45.25	**8.** _____
80	11	**9.** _____	$37.80	**10.** _____

Complete the table. Assume that 1 day = 8 hours.

Time Worked	Number of Electricians	Hourly Labor Rates	Total Labor Charge
$6\frac{1}{2}$ hours	1; 1 assistant	$21.00; $15.00	**11.** _____
15 hours	1; 2 assistants	$18.73; $12.00	**12.** _____
$12\frac{3}{4}$ hours	1; 2 assistants	$37.25; $25.85	**13.** _____
5 days	2; 2 assistants	$27.45; $18.50	**14.** _____
2 days 3 hours	2; 2 assistants	$38.35; $27.50	**15.** _____

Find the total cost of the job. Assume labor charges of $28.50 per hour for 1 electrician.

16. Parts: 800 ft #12 wire at $26.79 per 100 ft

400 ft #8 wire at $19.85 per 100 ft

12 outlet boxes at $7.45 each

6 receptacles at $5.35 each

6 outlet covers at $1.19 each

Labor: $7\frac{3}{4}$ hours

Total cost: _____

17. Parts: 300 ft #14 wire at $31.95 per 100 ft

5 junction boxes at $9.50 each

12 switches at $4.87 each

2 dimmers at $3.95 each

25 insulators at 16¢ each

Labor: $5\frac{1}{2}$ hours

Total cost: _____

18. Parts: 600 ft #10 wire at $23.65 per 100 ft

4 junction boxes at $10.15 each

11 switches at $4.95 each

3 dimmers at $4.25 each

22 insulators at 18¢ each

Labor: $6\frac{1}{2}$ hours

Total cost: _____

19. Parts: 400 ft #16 wire at $20.10 per 100 ft

300 ft #12 wire at $27.85 per ft

15 outlet boxes at $7.65 each

8 receptacles at $5.45 each

7 outlet covers at $1.25 each

Labor: $5\frac{3}{4}$ hours

Total cost: _____

Problem Solving Application: Surveyor

Juan Soldana is a surveyor. By measuring angles and certain distances that can be conveniently measured, he is able to calculate distances that cannot be directly measured.

Juan uses an instrument called a **transit** to measure angles. A transit is a telescope set on a three-legged stand. The transit also includes two protractors—one for measuring angles in a horizontal plane and the other for measuring angles in a vertical plane.

There are two facts about right triangles that help Juan perform his job.

- In any right triangle with a 30° angle, the side opposite that angle is $\frac{1}{2}$ of the length of the side opposite the 90° angle.

- In any right triangle with a 37° angle, the side opposite that angle is about $\frac{3}{5}$ of the length of the side opposite the 90° angle.

The Mathematics of Trades and Professions, SV 9780547625560

Name _____ Date _____

Find *n*. Remember to estimate whenever you use your calculator.

1.

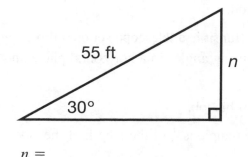

55 ft

n

30°

n = _____

2.

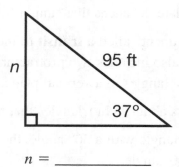

n

95 ft

37°

n = _____

3.

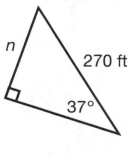

n

270 ft

37°

n = _____

4.

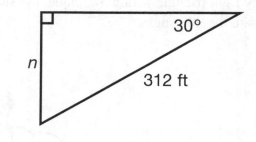

30°

n

312 ft

n = _____

5.

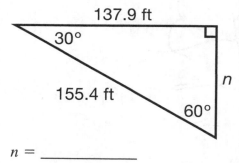

137.9 ft

30°

155.4 ft

n

60°

n = _____

6.

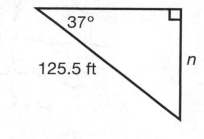

37°

125.5 ft

n

n = _____

7.

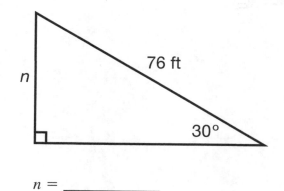

76 ft

n

30°

n = _____

8.

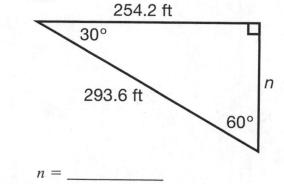

254.2 ft

30°

n

293.6 ft

60°

n = _____

Painting

Sam and Rick Owens are professional **painting contractors**. They need to order the correct amount of paint and to estimate the costs of jobs.

One gallon of most interior paint covers about 400 square ft with 1 coat.

Example 1: Sam and Rick have been contracted to paint two 11 ft by 30 ft walls. Each wall contains two 3 ft by 5 ft windows and a 3 ft by 7 ft door. Sam and Rick will use 2 coats of paint. How many gallons of paint will they need? At $12.75 per gallon, how much will the paint cost?

Step 1   Find the area to be painted.

- Find the total area. 2×11 ft $\times 30$ ft $= 660$ square ft

- Find the unpainted area. 4×3 ft $\times 5$ ft $= 60$ square ft
$$+\ 2 \times 3 \text{ ft} \times 7 \text{ ft} = 42 \text{ square ft}$$
$$102 \text{ square ft}$$

- Subtract to find the painted area.
  $660 - 102 = 558$ square ft

- Multiply to find the area for 2 coats of paint.
  $2 \times 558 = 1{,}116$ square ft

Step 2   Divide to find the number of gallons needed.
1,116 square ft $\div$ 400 square ft per gallon $= 2.79$ gallons
Sam and Rick will need to buy 3 gallons of paint.

Step 3   Multiply to find the cost.
3 gallons $\times$ $12.75 per gallon $=$ $38.25

The paint will cost $38.25.

The Mathematics of Trades and Professions, SV 9780547625560

Example 2: Sam and Rick usually work together and charge $20.00 per hour each for their labor. It took them $3\frac{1}{2}$ hours to paint the 2 walls. What was the labor cost?

THINK: 2 people $\times$ $3\frac{1}{2}$ $\times$ $20.00 per hour

Multiply $2 \times 3\frac{1}{2} \times \$20 = \$140.00$

Their labor charge was $140.00.

Example 3: Before getting the job, Sam and Rick must give the customer an estimate on how much the work will cost. For this job, Sam and Rick quoted a price of $180. Did they stay below their estimate or did they go over?

| Step 1 | Add the cost of paint and the labor charge.
$38.25 + $140.00 = $178.25

| Step 2 | Compare the actual cost and the estimate.
$178.25 < $180.00

Sam and Rick finished the job below their estimated price.

Think About It

1. Why does a gallon of interior paint usually cover more area than a gallon of exterior paint?

_____

_____

_____

_____

Practice

Remember to estimate whenever you use your calculator.

Complete the table. Assume that each wall contains two 3 ft by 5 ft windows and a 3 ft by 7 ft door. Assume that paint costs $16.50 per gal.

Dimensions of Wall(s)	Total Area	Unpainted Area	Painted Area	Number of Coats	Number of Gallons Needed	Cost of Paint
One 9 ft by 12 ft	1. _____	2. _____	3. _____	1	4. _____	5. _____
One 15 ft by 25 ft	6. _____	7. _____	8. _____	1	9. _____	10. _____
One 8 ft by 16 ft	11. _____	12. _____	13. _____	2	14. _____	15. _____
Two 24 ft by 40 ft	16. _____	17. _____	18. _____	2	19. _____	20. _____
Two 40 ft by 70 ft	21. _____	22. _____	23. _____	2	24. _____	25. _____

Complete the table. Assume that 1 day = 8 hours.

Number of Painters	Time Worked per Painter	Cost per Hour per Painter	Total Labor Cost
2	12 hours	$14.00	26. _____
5	$2\frac{1}{2}$ days	$16.50	27. _____
3	4 days 3 hours	$21.15	28. _____
12	5 days	$18.75	29. _____

Name _____ Date _____

Use the diagram of the barn for Exercises 30-35.

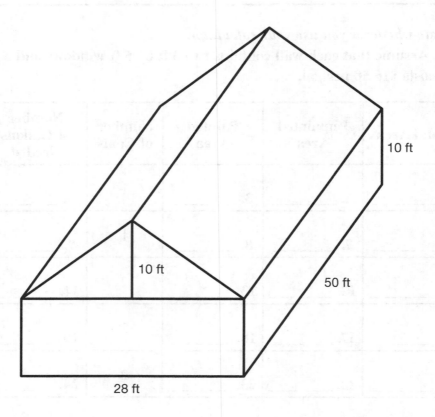

10 ft

10 ft

50 ft

28 ft

What is the area of:

30. the longer side? _____

31. the shorter side? _____

32. the triangular rise? _____

33. 2 longer sides, 1 shorter side, and the triangular rise? _____

34. One gallon of exterior paint covers about 250 square ft. How many gallons of paint will be needed to cover the area in problem 33? _____

35. How many gallons of paint will be needed to cover the area in problem 33 with two coats?

_____

The Mathematics of Trades and Professions, SV 9780547625560

Problem Solving Application: Carpet Installer

Charles Monet is a carpet installer. The ability to measure accurately is important in wall-to-wall carpeting. Often, a room may consist of more than one rectangular section. Sometimes several rooms and a hallway are carpeted with the same type of carpet.

Find the number of square yards of carpeting needed.

1.

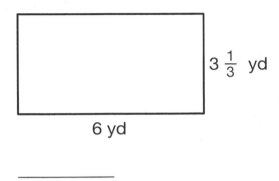

_____

2.

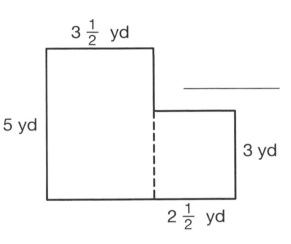

3.

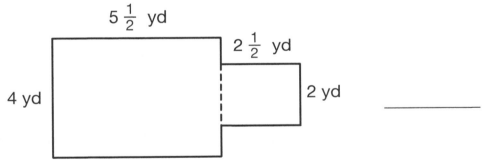

_____

4.

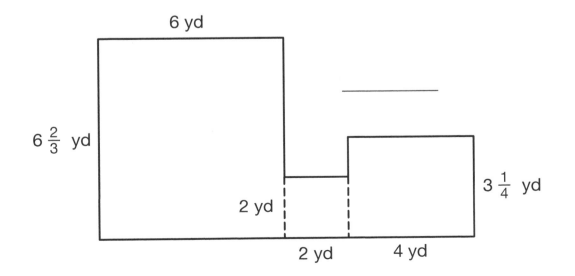

Name _____   Date _____

Solve.

5. Charles installs wall-to-wall carpeting in a rectangular room that is 6.5 yd long and 4.0 yd wide. What is the area covered by the carpet? _____

6. In the same house, Charles carpets a rectangular room 5.8 yd long and 4.2 yd wide. How much less is the area covered by this carpet than the area covered in problem 5? _____

7. During a period of one week, Charles worked a total of 35 hours. Of this time, 24.5 hours were spent installing carpets. 10.5 hours were spent traveling to and from the clients' homes. What percent of Charles' time was spent traveling? _____

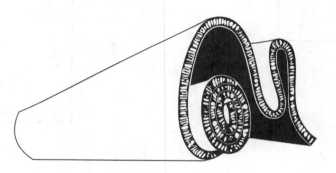

Charles' cousin, Ann, decides to buy wall-to-wall carpeting for a rectangular room 21 ft long and 18 ft wide.

8. What is the area of the floor in square yards? _____

9. When Ann orders the carpeting, should she order an amount that is less than, equal to, or greater than the area of the floor? Why?

_____

_____

_____

The Mathematics of Trades and Professions, SV 9780547625560

Masonry

Carla Mendez is a **mason**. She uses bricks, cement blocks, and mortar to construct walls and fireplaces. Masons use mathematics to order materials, to compute the cost of jobs, and to complete projects accurately and according to plans.

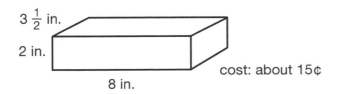

$3\frac{1}{2}$ in.

2 in.

8 in.

cost: about 15¢

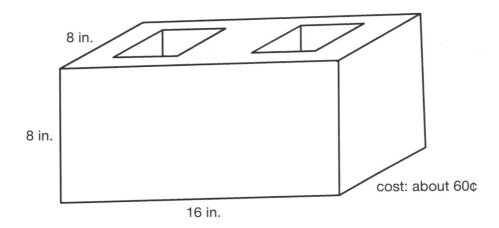

8 in.

8 in.

16 in.

cost: about 60¢

Masons use standard-sized bricks that measure 8 in. by 2 in. by $3\frac{1}{2}$ in. They use standard-sized concrete blocks that measure 16 in. by 8 in. by 8 in.

Example 1: Carla is contracted to construct a 249-square-ft brick façade on the front of a new house. If Carla uses 9 bricks per square ft, how many bricks should she order? At 15¢ per brick, how much will the bricks cost?

| Step 1 | Multiply to find the number of bricks.

249 square ft × 9 bricks/square ft = 2,241 bricks

Carla should order 2,241 bricks.

| Step 2 | Multiply to find the cost.

2,241 bricks × $0.15 per brick = $336.15

The bricks will cost $336.15.

Example 2: Carla has found that mixing 2 bags of cement with 5 cubic ft of sand makes enough mortar for about 100 square ft of brickwork. How many bags of cement will she need for the 249-square-ft job in Example 1? At $6.75 per bag, how much will the cement cost?

| Step 1 | Use a proportion to find the number of bags.
Round up the answer.
THINK: 2 bags is to 100 square ft as *n* bags is to 249 square ft.

$$\frac{2 \text{ bags}}{100 \text{ square ft}} = \frac{n \text{ bags}}{249 \text{ square ft}}$$

$100n = 2 \times 249$
$100n = 498$
$n = 498 \div 100 = 4.98 \approx 5$

Carla will need 5 bags of cement.

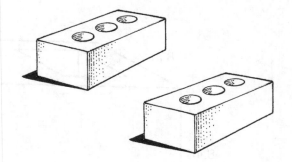

| Step 2 | Multiply to find the cost.
5 bags × $6.75 per bag = $33.75

The cement will cost $33.75.

Think About It

1. Why do masons usually order more bricks than their computations indicate?

_____

_____

_____

2. Why are many fireplaces constructed primarily of cement blocks with bricks placed only on the visible parts?

_____

_____

_____

Practice

Remember to estimate whenever you use your calculator.

Complete the table. Assume that concrete blocks cost 60¢ each and that you use 10 blocks per square yard.

Total Area	Number of Blocks Needed	Cost of Blocks
12 square yd	1. _____	2. _____
38 square yd	3. _____	4. _____
327 square yd	5. _____	6. _____
1,624 square yd	7. _____	8. _____

Complete the table. Assume that bricks cost 15¢ each and that you use 9 bricks per square ft. Assume that you need 2 bags of cement for 100 square ft and that cement costs $7.25 per bag.

Total Area	Number of Bricks Needed	Cost of Bricks	Number of Bags of Cement Needed	Cost of Cement
12 square ft	9. _____	10. _____	11. _____	12. _____
38 square ft	13. _____	14. _____	15. _____	16. _____
327 square ft	17. _____	18. _____	19. _____	20. _____
1,624 square ft	21. _____	22. _____	23. _____	24. _____

Name _____ Date _____

Use the diagram of the house for problems 25-27.

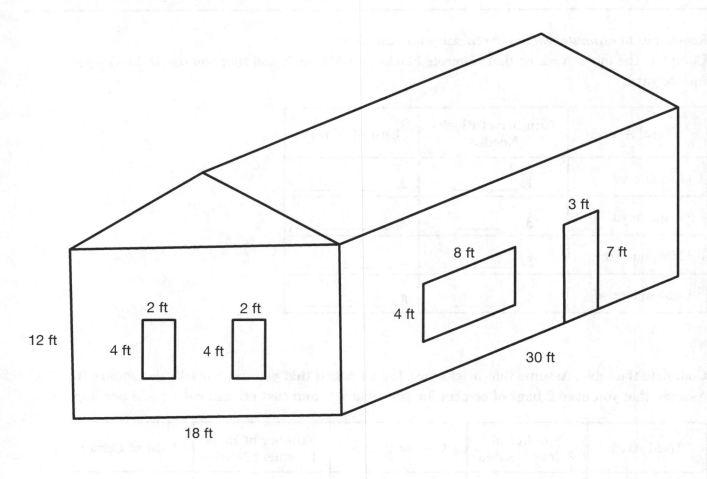

25. What is the area of the longer side of the house, excluding windows and doors? _____ The shorter side? _____

26. At 9 bricks per square ft, how many bricks will be needed to face the 2 visible sides? _____

27. At 2 bags of cement per 100 square ft, how many bags of cement will be needed for the job in problem 26? _____

Problem Solving Strategy: Drawing a Diagram

Situation:

Mike owns a landscape-contracting company. Mike's crew built a fence around a square piece of land that measured 4 yards on each side. The fence posts were placed 1 yard apart. How many poles did Mike need?

Strategy:

Drawing a diagram can help you to solve a problem.

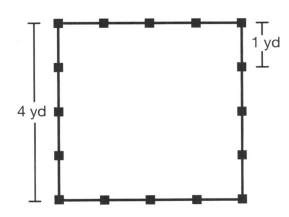

Applying the Strategy:

| Step 1 | Draw a square. |

| Step 2 | Mark the 4 corner posts. |

| Step 3 | Mark posts 1 yd apart. |

| Step 4 | Count the number of posts needed. |

Mike needed 16 posts.

Think About It

Mike designed a flower bed for a customer. The first row of flowers was red. The second row of flowers was yellow. This pattern was repeated.

1. What would you draw to help you see the flower bed?

_____

_____

2. What color were the flowers in the ninth row?

_____

The Mathematics of Trades and Professions, SV 9780547625560

Practice

Fill in the missing numbers from the diagrams to solve the problem.

1. Mike's crew planted a row of pine trees on the 60-ft side of Mr. Wesley's yard. A pine was planted every 10 ft. How many pines were planted?

   _____

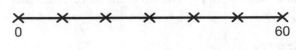

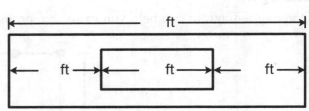

2. A 12-ft-long flower bed was cut into a rectangular lawn. The lawn is 32 ft long. The flower bed is in the center of the lawn. How many feet of lawn are on each side of the flower bed? _____

Solve the problem by drawing a diagram.

3. An azalea garden contains 49 azaleas, 7 in each row. The center and end azaleas in each row are pink. How many pink azaleas are there in all? _____

4. A row of trees was planted along Maple Drive. The length of the row was 148 ft. A tree was planted every $18\frac{1}{2}$ ft. How many trees were planted? _____

5. Mike built a fence around a rectangular garden that was 16 yd long and 12 yd wide. The posts were placed 2 yd apart. How many posts did he need? _____

6. A rectangular lawn contains three 7-ft-square flower beds. There is a border of 3 ft between each flower bed and the perimeter of the plot. How long is the plot? _____

Decision Making: Quality and Quantity vs. Price

Many goods are produced and sold in a variety of qualities. It is common to see items advertised as "Good" or "Everyday Grade" at lower prices and "Deluxe" or "Our Best" at higher prices.

Problem A

Sandra's flooring contractor showed her samples of 3 grades of vinyl flooring for her 3 yd by 4 yd kitchen. She needs to decide which grade to order.

GOOD VINYL FLOORING	STYLISH VINYL FLOORING	DELUXE VINYL FLOORING
$8.99/square yd	$10.99/square yd No-Wax Finish	$12.99/square yd Never needs waxing 10-year guarantee

Decision-Making Factors

• Cost   • Quality   • Maintenance/upkeep   • Guarantees

Decision-Making Comparisons

Compare the 3 options by completing the table.

Factor	Good Flooring	Stylish Flooring	Deluxe Flooring
Total Cost	1. _____	$131.88	2. _____
Quality	Average	3. _____	4. _____
Maintenance	Needs waxing	5. _____	6. _____
Guarantees	7. _____	None	8. _____

Making the Decisions

Which flooring should Sandra order:

9. If cost were the only factor? _____

10. If quality were the only factor? _____

11. If ease of maintenance *and* cost were important factors? _____

12. Which flooring could she expect to last the longest? _____
    Why?

    _____

    _____

13. How much could Sandra save by using the Good flooring instead of the Deluxe flooring to do the kitchen? _____

    What could cause her not really to save this much over the next 10 years?

    _____

    _____

14. Which type of flooring would you order? _____ Why?

    _____

    _____

    _____

The Mathematics of Trades and Professions, SV 9780547625560

Problem B

Many contractors have the opportunity to save money by **buying in bulk**. A mason might find brick available at 3 different rates, depending on the quantity he orders. He must decide the best way to order the bricks based on the following pricing information.

LOOSE BRICKS 16¢ each	BRICKS ON A PALLET $49.00 (400 bricks/pallet)	TRUCKLOAD OF BRICKS $430.00 (10 pallets/truckload)

Decision-Making Factors

- Cost
- Availability of space
- Minimum purchase/number needed
- Ease of transport

Decision-Making Comparisons

Compare the 3 options by completing the table.

Factor	Loose	Pallet	Truckload
Cost per Brick	16¢	15. _____	16. _____
Minimum Purchase of Bricks	None	17. _____	18. _____
Need for Storage	19. _____	Moderate	20. _____
Ease of Transport	21. _____	22. _____	Low

The Mathematics of Trades and Professions, SV 9780547625560

Making the Decision

Which way should the mason order the bricks:

23. If cost were the only factor? _____

24. If he only needs 150 bricks? _____

25. If transportation is not a factor and he needs 500 bricks? _____

26. How much can the mason save by ordering a pallet instead of 400 loose bricks? _____

27. How much can the mason save by ordering a truckload instead of 10 pallets? _____

28. What is the least expensive way to order 2,000 bricks? _____

    How much will they cost? _____

29. Suppose the mason needs 3,600 bricks for a job. What is the best way to order the bricks? _____

    How much will they cost? _____

30. What hidden costs might be involved before assuming that buying bricks by the truckload is least expensive? _____

31. Which way would you order the bricks if you needed 300? _____

    3,000? _____

    5,000? _____

    Why?

    _____

    _____

    _____

Problem Solving Application: Draftsperson

Ellen Jessup is a draftsperson. As part of her job, she makes mechanical drawings that show how to construct parts of machines. The drawings must be very precise. Otherwise, the parts of the machines will not be correct.

Find the measurement to the nearest tenth of a centimeter.

1.

    The actual machine part is 2.5 times as long as the drawing. What is the length of the actual part?

2.

    A metal strip is 4.5 times as long as the drawing. What is the length of the actual metal strip?

3.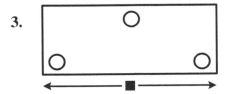

    How long is the drawing?

4.

    What is the diameter of the washer?

Sometimes, large drawings are made for small machine parts. In problems 5–8, the actual part is 0.25 as long as the dimension of the given drawing.

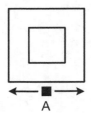

A

C

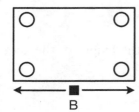

B

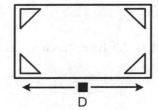

D

Find the missing numbers to the nearest tenth of a centimeter. Remember to estimate whenever you use your calculator.

	Drawing	**Length of Drawing**	**Length of Part**
5.	A	_____	_____
6.	B	_____	_____
7.	C	_____	_____
8.	D	_____	_____

Money Tips 1

Service contracts on many items can save you money on repairs and maintenance.

Let's Look at the Facts

Many new items include a **warranty** that covers defects and repairs during the first 90 days, the first year, and so forth. After the warranty expires, paying 1 annual **service contract** fee on a computer, for example, could save you money.

APT-4F PERSONAL COMPUTER SYSTEM	
(Service Contract--$350 per year)	
Parts Replacement Charges	**Service and Labor Charges**
Replacement keys $12	Service call. $75
Disc drive mechanism $15	Labor (repair time, per hour) $35
Printer cable $40	Maintenance check and system cleaning $100
Keyboard and mouse $55	Pickup and delivery for in-shop repairs. $50
Printer cartridge $60	Reinstallation of Programs . . . $45
Interface Unit. $90	
Monitor. $200	

Let's Discuss Why

1. When would you be more likely to have ongoing or increasing problems with your personal computer (PC)?

   _____

   _____

2. For every call to your home or office, you pay a service charge regardless of whether any work is done or not. How much would it cost just to call in a repairperson 5 times in 1 year?

   _____

3. Your PC needs an overall cleaning twice a year. Each call requires $1\frac{1}{2}$ hours of labor. What would this cost per year?

_____

_____

4. Your PC was repaired 10 times last year. You had bought a service contract for last year. Therefore, what was the most that each service call actually cost you?

_____

_____

Let's See What You Would Do

5. You bought a service contract on your PC for 2 years. In the first year, no repairs were needed. In the second year, all major parts were replaced, and the computer was cleaned twice and taken into the shop twice. Four service calls were made, requiring 12 hours of labor. Compare the total cost with the cost of the service plan.

_____

_____

_____

6. Look around your home, school, or office. On how many items could you take out a service contract?

_____

www.harcourtschoolsupply.com
74
Part II
The Mathematics of Trades and Professions, SV 9780547625560

Calculator: Discounts and Add-ons

You can use a calculator to find the total cost of an item selling at a discount or one that includes an add-on such as sales tax.

A drill that regularly sells for $64 is being sold at a 15% discount. What is the sale price?

	Procedure	**Calculator Entry**	**Calculator Display**
Step 1	Enter the regular price.	6 4	64.
Step 2	Enter the − key.	−	64.
Step 3	Enter the discount rate.	1 5 %	54.4

The sale price is $54.40.

Try this on your calculator. On some calculators, you may need to enter the = key after the % key. If your calculator does not have a % key, multiply 64 by the decimal equivalent of 15% (.15) and subtract this amount from the original price.

The Mathematics of Trades and Professions, SV 9780547625560

What is the total cost of a $325 Tablet PC on which a 6% sales tax must be paid?

	Procedure	**Calculator Entry**	**Calculator Display**
Step 1	Enter the regular price.	3 2 5	325.
Step 2	Enter the ⎡ + ⎤ key.	+	325.
Step 3	Enter the sales tax rate.	6 %	344.5

Try this on your calculator. On some calculators, you may need to enter the ⎡ = ⎤ key after the ⎡ % ⎤ key. If your calculator does not have a ⎡ % ⎤ key, multiply 325 by the decimal equivalent of 6% (.06) and add this amount from the original price.

Use a calculator to compute.

1. Regular price: $300

   Discount rate: 12%

   Sale price: _____

2. Regular price: $50

   Discount rate: 21.5%

   Sale price: _____

3. Regular price: $175

   Sales tax: 6.5%

   Total cost: _____

Use a calculator to solve.

4. A power saw that lists for $85 is on sale at a 25% discount. What is the sale price? _____

5. What is the total price of a $480 air conditioner in a state with a 7.5% sales tax? _____

Part II Review

Vocabulary

Choose the letter of the word(s) that completes the sentence.

1. Carpenters usually pay for lumber by the _____.

   a. Piece   **b.** Board foot   **c.** Ton

2. The amount of paint needed is most dependent on _____.

   a. Length   **b.** Area   **c.** Volume

3. A skilled person who works with bricks, cement blocks, and mortar is called a(n) _____.

   a. Plumber   **b.** Electrical contractor   **c.** Mason

4. Compared to new residential construction, residential renovation is usually _____.

   a. More expensive   **b.** Less expensive   **c.** About the same price

Skills

Find the answer.

5. At $80 per square ft, how much will it cost to add a 16 ft by 24 ft playroom to a house? _____

6. At $100 per square ft, how much will it cost to renovate 35,000 square ft of abandoned factory space? _____

7. At 32¢ per board ft, what will be the cost of 25 16-ft-long pieces of 2 in. by 10 in. lumber?

   _____

8. How thick is a pipe with an inside diameter of $2\frac{3}{8}$ in. and an outside diameter of $2\frac{3}{4}$ in.?

   _____

9. If you need 25 12-ft sections of pipe, how many 100-ft coils do you need to buy? _____

10. A plumber charges $28 per hour for labor. How much will a 24-hour job cost? _____

11. An electrician averages 75 ft of wire per room when wiring a new home. How many 100-ft coils of wire should be purchased for a 6-room house?

_____

12. An electrician charges $29.75 per hour for his own labor and $18.75 per hour for his assistant's labor. What is the total labor charge for a $6\frac{1}{2}$ hour job?

_____

13. What is the area to be painted on two 16 ft by 30 ft walls that each contain one 3 ft by 5 ft window and a 3 ft by 7 ft door? _____

14. If a gallon of paint covers about 350 square ft, how much paint is needed to put 2 coats on the walls in problem 13? _____

15. At 9 bricks per square ft, how many bricks are needed to construct a brick façade on a $9\frac{1}{2}$ ft by 27 ft wall? _____

16. At 15¢ per brick, how much will it cost to construct the wall in problem 15? _____

Part II Test

Find the cost.

1. 2,200 square ft of construction at $80 per square ft _____

2. 600 square ft of renovation at $100 per square ft _____

3. Ten 18-ft-long pieces of 2 in. by 4 in. lumber at 47¢ per board ft _____

4. Fifteen 20-ft sections of pipe at 15¢ per ft _____

5. 400 ft of electrical cable wire at $42.75 per 100 ft _____

6. 18 gal of paint at $13.99 per gal _____

Solve.

7. What is the inside diameter of a sewer pipe with a $6\frac{1}{4}$ in. outside diameter and a $\frac{5}{16}$-in. thickness? _____

8. How many 100-ft coils of wire are needed for a 7-room house if an electrician uses an average of 75 ft per room? _____

The Mathematics of Trades and Professions, SV 9780547625560

9. An electrician charges $32.50 per hour for her labor and $24.75 per hour for her assistant's labor. What is the labor charge for a $9\frac{1}{2}$ hour job? _____

10. What is the area to be painted on two 9 ft by 20 ft walls that each contain two 3 ft by 5 ft windows and a 3 ft by 7 ft door? _____

11. Paint costs $15.99 per gallon, and 1 gallon covers 400 square ft. How much will it cost to put 2 coats on the walls in problem 10? _____

12. At 9 bricks per square ft and 18¢ per brick, what will it cost to add a brick face to the 15 ft by 36 ft side of a house? _____

Find the cost of the materials.

13. Twelve 18-ft-long pieces of 2 in. by 4 in. lumber at 29.5¢ per board ft; 8 sheets paneling at $8.99 per sheet; 2 lb nails at 85¢ per lb _____

14. 175 ft copper pipe at 18¢ per ft; 100 ft plastic pipe at 26¢ per ft; 8 plastic elbows at 69¢ each; 10 couplers at 49¢ each _____

Solve the problem by drawing a diagram.

15. Fencing was built around a 6 yard by 6 yard piece of land. The posts were 1 yard apart. How many posts were there? _____

16. There are 18 rows in a garden. The first row is white, the second row is pink, and the third row is red. This pattern is repeated. What color is the 15th row? _____

Part III:
Other Professions

Pre-Skills Test

Compute.

1. $8\frac{1}{2} \times \$12.20 =$ _____

2. $17\frac{3}{4} \times \$18.50 =$ _____

3. $56\frac{1}{2} \times \$25.74 =$ _____

4. $(4 \times \$56.80) + (5 \times \$284.50) =$ _____

5. $(15 \times \$14.80) + (8 \times \$37.60) =$ _____

Divide. Round to the nearest whole number.

6. $\$1,000 \div \$63.49 =$ _____

7. $\$250 \div \$7.65 =$ _____

8. $\$750 \div \$85.60 =$ _____

9. $8\frac{3}{4} \div 1\frac{3}{4} =$ _____

10. $15 \div 1\frac{1}{2} =$ _____

11. $13\frac{1}{2} \div 2\frac{1}{4} =$ _____

Solve for n.

12. $\frac{15}{120} = \frac{n}{800}$

$n =$ _____

13. $\frac{24}{90} = \frac{300}{n}$

$n =$ _____

14. $\frac{2}{125} = \frac{n}{5,000}$

$n =$ _____

Find the answer.

15. 1% of 2,400 _____

16. 2% of 360 _____

17. 5% of 6,700 _____

18. 3% of 175 _____

19. 15% of 4,000 _____

20. $1\frac{1}{2}$% of 500 _____

Name _____ Date _____

Complete.

21. 1 liter = _____ milliliters

22. 500 milliliters = _____ liters

23. 50 cubic centimeters = _____ milliliters

24. 1,000 milligrams = _____ grams

25. 3 grams = _____ milligrams

26. 1,000 cubic centimeters = _____ liters

Add or subtract.

27. 3 minutes 37 seconds + 8 minutes 51 seconds _____

28. 17 minutes 28 seconds + 4 minutes 43 seconds _____

29. 30 minutes − 14 minutes 23 seconds _____

30. 45 minutes − 8 minutes 12 seconds _____

Use the line graph for problems 31-37. How many bathing suits were bought during the months?

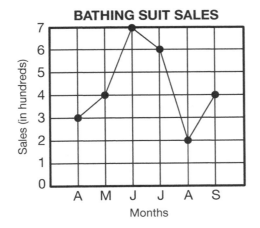

31. April _____

32. May _____

33. June _____

34. July _____

35. August _____

36. September _____

37. During which period of time was there the greatest increase in sales? _____

The Mathematics of Trades and Professions, SV 9780547625560

Advertising

Mathematics is used extensively in the advertising industry in designing ads and computing the cost of placing the ads in print publications, radio and television broadcasts, and on the Internet.

The cost of ads in newspapers is usually computed based on column-inches, or the number of columns wide the ad is by the number of inches long the ad runs.

Example 1: Fits-Well Shoe Store placed an ad for a sale in the local newspaper. The ad was 3 columns wide and ran $5\frac{1}{2}$ in. The newspaper charged $11.34 per column-inch. How much did it cost to run the ad for 1 day?

Step 1 | Multiply to find the column-inches.
$3 \times 5\frac{1}{2}$ in. $= 16\frac{1}{2}$

Step 2 | Multiply to find the cost.
THINK: $16\frac{1}{2} = 16.5$
$16.5 \times \$11.34 = \$187.11$

The ad cost $187.11.

Example 2: The Hoyt Agency designed an ad that was $8\frac{1}{2}$ in. wide and 11 in. long. How much did it cost to run the ad for 5 days if each column was $2\frac{1}{8}$ in. wide?

THINK: If each column was $2\frac{1}{8}$ in. wide, then 2 columns were $4\frac{1}{4}$ in. wide and 4 columns were $8\frac{1}{2}$ in. wide. So an $8\frac{1}{2}$ in. $\times$ 11 in. ad used 4 columns.

Step 1 | Multiply to find the column-inches.
4×11 in. $= 44$

Step 2 | Multiply to find the cost.
$44 \times \$11.34 \times 5$ days $= \$2,494.80$

It cost $2,494.80 to run the ad for 5 days.

Many newspapers have set rates for quarter-, half-, and full-page ads.

Example 3: An ad agency has a $1,500 budget for a client. For how many days can they run a half-page ad? If the ad were reduced in size, for how many days could they run a quarter-page ad?

AD RATES
Full page - $1,326.12
Half page - $667.53
Quarter page - $341.86

Step 1 Divide to find the half-page time.
$1,500 ÷ $667.53 = 2.24709

They could run the half-page ad for 2 days.

Step 2 Divide to find the quarter-page time.
$1,500 ÷ $341.86 = 4.387761

They could run the quarter-page ad for 4 days.

Think About It

1. Why is the cost of a full-page ad often so much greater in one newspaper than in another?

_____

_____

_____

_____

Practice

Remember to estimate whenever you use your calculator.

Complete the table. Assume that the cost per column-inch is $16.87.

Number of Columns	Number of Inches	Number of Column-Inches	Cost to Place Ad
1	$3\frac{1}{2}$	1. _____	2. _____
3	$7\frac{1}{4}$	3. _____	4. _____
2	$10\frac{3}{4}$	5. _____	6. _____
5	$14\frac{1}{4}$	7. _____	8. _____

Complete the table. Assume that each column is $1\frac{3}{4}$ in. wide and that the cost per column-inch is $23.48.

Ad Size (width by length)	Number of Column-Inches	Cost to Place Ad
$3\frac{1}{2}$ in. by 8 in.	9. _____	10. _____
$1\frac{3}{4}$ in. by $4\frac{1}{2}$ in.	11. _____	12. _____
$5\frac{1}{4}$ in. by $10\frac{3}{4}$ in.	13. _____	14. _____
$8\frac{3}{4}$ in. by $8\frac{3}{4}$ in.	15. _____	16. _____

Use the ad rates on page 85 to solve.

17. With a $2,500 budget, for how many days could you run a half-page ad? _____

18. With a $4,000 budget, for how many days could you run a quarter-page ad? _____

19. Each page in a newspaper is 6 columns wide by 20 in. long. How many column-inches are there in a quarter-page ad? _____

At $14.87 per column-inch, how much will the ad cost? _____

20. Each page in a local newspaper is 8 columns wide by 14 in. long. How many column-inches are in a half-page ad? _____

At $8.31 per column inch, how much will the ad cost? _____

Problem Solving Application: Advertising Executive

Michelle Morales works for a small advertising agency. She is the Account Executive for a car manufacturer. It is her job to make and present an advertising campaign for the new Augusta sports car.

Michelle used a **divided-bar graph** in her presentation to the client.

Television $\frac{2}{5}$	Radio $\frac{1}{4}$	Magazines $\frac{1}{4}$	Direct Mail $\frac{1}{10}$

Use the divided-bar graph to answer problems 1–10.

What part of the advertising budget is devoted to:

1. Radio? _____

2. Television? _____

3. Magazines? _____

4. Direct mail? _____

5. Which type of advertising received the smallest part of the budget?

   _____

6. Which types of advertising were allotted equal parts of the budget?

   _____

The Mathematics of Trades and Professions, SV 9780547625560

Solve.

7. Use the 20 by 5 rectangle below to show the Augusta graph using decimals instead of fractions.

8. What is the sum of the decimals in the graph for problem 7? _____

9. The part of the budget allotted for television is how many times as great as the part allotted for direct mail? (Use the decimals in your graph.) _____

10. Suppose a total of $8,500,000 will be used for the Augusta campaign. How much money will be used for each of the four types of advertising?

   Radio? _____

   Television? _____

   Magazine? _____

   Direct mail? _____

11. Why do you think Michelle has chosen to spend more money on television advertising than on any other types of advertising?

   _____

   _____

12. Which types of magazines would be best for advertising a new sports car?

   _____

   Why?

   _____

   _____

Sales

Salespeople in all industries use graphs to display important sales data. These graphs provide information quickly and in a visually pleasing way. Graphs of sales data are often used to evaluate the success of past activities and to plan future activities.

Line graphs are very useful for showing trends over time.

A large discount appliance chain graphed the sales of 2 major brands of televisions during each month of the year.

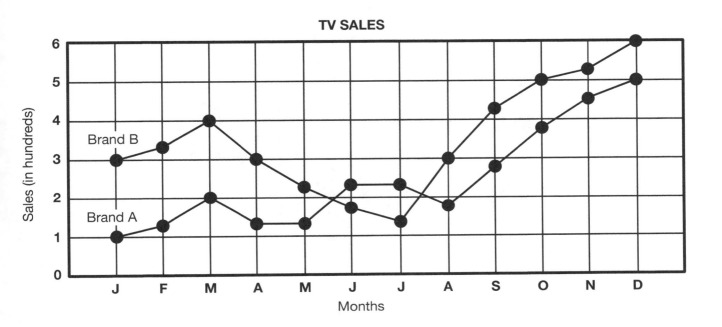

Example 1: For which months were sales of Brand A greater than those for Brand B?

The Brand A line is higher than the Brand B line in only June and July.

Name _____ Date _____

Example 2: The store ran a major advertising campaign for Brand A during May and June. Did the campaign appear to have been successful?

Since sales for Brand A surpassed those for Brand B following the ad campaign, it looks like the campaign was successful in promoting sales.

Example 3: How would you explain the higher sales of both brands during November and December?

It is likely that many televisions were purchased as gifts during the holiday season, when many stores make 30% to 50% of their annual sales.

Name _____   Date _____

1. What are some advantages of using a graph rather than a table with the same data?

_____

_____

2. Given the TV sales trends in the graph, when might you best schedule a major ad campaign to boost sales of Brand A? Brand B?

_____

_____

Practice

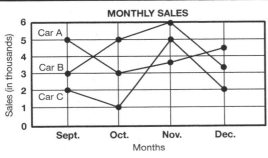

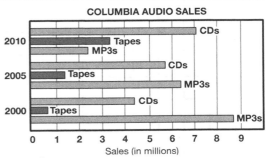

Write 3 conclusions that can be drawn from the data in the graph.

  1. Graph 1:

_____

_____

_____

  2. Graph 2:

_____

_____

Suggest 1 action, including its timing, that you would use to boost sales in:

  3. Cars.

_____

  4. MP3s, CDs, Tapes.

_____

The Mathematics of Trades and Professions, SV 9780547625560

Name _____ Date _____

SALES		
Week	**Shoes**	**Sneakers**
1	543	389
2	390	137
3	817	580
4	645	244
5	287	256

(Hint: Label the vertical scale in hundreds to 900.)

PURCHASES		
Year	**Hotdogs**	**Burgers**
1985	4,385	3,189
1986	6,408	4,890
1987	5,724	5,836
1988	4,233	7,492
1989	4,879	8,943

(Hint: Label the vertical scale in thousands to 9,000.)

Make a line graph for the data in the tables.

5.

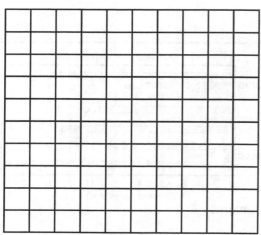

6.

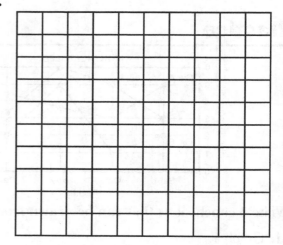

Write 3 conclusions that can be drawn from the data in:

7. Problem 5:

_____

_____

8. Problem 6:

_____

_____

Suggest 1 action, including its timing, that you would use to boost sales in:

9. Shoes:

_____

10. Hot dogs:

_____

Problem Solving Application: Store Owner

Rosa Aquino owns a neighborhood clothing store. She buys merchandise at a certain cost and then sells it to people in small quantities.

Rosa must pay certain expenses such as rent, telephone, and electricity. To meet these expenses and make a profit, she must sell her merchandise for a greater amount than it costs.

To do this, Rosa marks up the merchandise at a rate of 50%. That is, the **markup** is 50% of the cost. The **selling price** is found by adding the markup to the cost. What would Rosa sell a pair of slacks for if they cost her $18?

Step 1 | Find the amount of the markup.
THINK: 50% = 0.50
0.50 × $18 = $9

Step 2 | Add to find the selling price.
$18 + $9 = $27

So, Rosa would sell the pair of slacks for $27.

Find the markup and the selling price. Remember to estimate whenever you use your calculator.

Item	Cost of Merchandise	Percent of Markup	Amount of Markup	Selling Price
1. A	$24	50%	_____	_____
2. B	$156	30%	_____	_____
3. C	$25	40%	_____	_____
4. D	$60	45%	_____	_____
5. E	$8.50	43%	_____	_____
6. F	$19.75	36%	_____	_____
7. G	$25.20	$33\frac{1}{3}$%	_____	_____
8. H	$18.50	37.5%	_____	_____

Solve. Rosa buys one type of shirt at $192 per dozen.

9. What is the cost per shirt? _____

10. What is the selling price per shirt if the markup is 50%? _____

Travel

International travelers and travel agents frequently turn to mathematics when they use **exchange rates** to convert dollars to other currencies, or other currencies to dollars. Travelers also use exchange rates to compute the equivalent value of an item in 2 different currencies.

Exchange Rates	
$1 U.S. =	0.709 euro (Europe)
	0.605 pound (United Kingdom)
	0.977 dollar (Canada)
	11.959 pesos (Mexico)
	44.785 rupees (India)
	81.705 yen (Japan)

Example 1: Before leaving for France, you converted $600 in U.S. currency to euros. How many euros did you receive?

THINK: $1 U.S. = 0.709 euro

Step 1 | Use a proportion.

THINK: $1 is to 0.709 euro as $600 is to n euros.

$$\frac{\$1}{0.709 \text{ euro}} = \frac{\$600}{n \text{ euros}}$$

$$n = 600 \times 0.709 = 425.40$$

Step 2 | Round down.

$$425.40 \approx 425$$

You received 425 euros.

Example 2: When you were in Japan, your hotel room was billed at a rate of 5,882 yen per night. How much was this in U.S. dollars?

THINK: $1 U.S. = 81.705 yen

Step 1 Use a proportion.

THINK: $1 is to 81.705 yen as n dollars is to 5,882 yen.

$$\frac{\$1}{81.705} = \frac{n}{5,882} \text{ yen}$$

$$81.705n = 5,882$$

$$n = 5,882 \div 81.705 = 71.9906982$$

Step 1 Round down.

$$71.9906982 \approx 71.99$$

In U.S. dollars, the room was $71.99 per night.

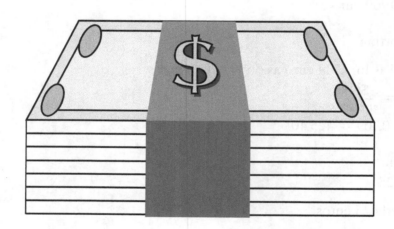

Think About It

1. The dollar/yen exchange rate fluctuated widely between 120 yen to the dollar and 160 yen to the dollar. When would have been the worst time to buy a Japanese import car? Why?

_____

_____

_____

_____

Practice

Remember to estimate whenever you use your calculator.
Using the exchange rates shown on page 95, calculate the value of $750 U.S. in:

1. Euros _____
2. Canadian dollars _____
3. Yen _____
4. Pesos _____
5. Rupees _____
6. Pounds _____

Complete the table.

Item	Value in U.S. Dollars	Value in Other Currency
Watch	$75	7. _____ pesos
Dress	$260	8. _____ euros
Camera	$195	9. _____ yen
Jewelry	$39.95	10. _____ rupees
Clarinet	$550	11. _____ Canadian dollars
Television	$495	12. _____ pounds

Convert to dollars. Use the exchange rates on page 95.

13. Perfume for 125 euros _____

14. Clothes for 79 Canadian dollars _____

15. An umbrella for 10 euros _____

16. A television for 45,000 yen _____

17. A car for 23,000 euros _____

18. Furniture for 12,000 pesos _____

19. Souvenirs for 101 Canadian dollars _____

20. A painting for 455 rupees _____

| Extension | The Effects of Changing Exchange Rates |

An Army corporal stationed in Germany is paid $484 per week. What is the impact on the corporal's wages when the exchange rate decreases from 0.709 to 0.652 euro to the dollar?

Procedure: **1.** Convert the wages to euros at the old rate. _____

2. Convert the wages to euros at the new rate. _____

3. Convert the decrease in euros to dollars at the old rate, that is, the loss in buying power expressed in dollars. _____

Manufacturing

A key component of all assembly lines and all manufacturing industries is **quality control**—that is, assuring the same high quality and consistency in each manufactured item. Quality control inspectors use **sampling techniques** and proportions in their ongoing efforts to assure quality goods for the buyer.

Example 1: A quality-control inspector pulls 1 out of every 150 light bulbs from the production line for testing. If the line produces 27,000 bulbs per day, how many are pulled for testing?

Use a proportion.

THINK: 1 is to 150 as n is to 27,000.

$$\frac{1}{150} = \frac{n}{27,000}$$

$$150n = 27,000$$

$$n = 27,000 \div 150 = 180$$

The inspector pulls 180 light bulbs for testing.

Inspectors use sampling to predict the number of defective items.

Example 2: On a given day, a quality-control inspector found 2 defective bulbs out of 115 that were tested. If the day's total production was 22,500 bulbs, predict how many were defective.

Use a proportion.

THINK: 2 is to 115 as n is to 22,500.

$$\frac{2 \text{ defective}}{115 \text{ tested}} = \frac{n \text{ defective}}{22,500 \text{ produced}}$$

$$115n = 2 \times 22,500 = 45,000$$

$$n = 45,000 \div 115 = 391.30434$$

You would predict that about 391 bulbs were defective.

Example 3: A company that produces toaster ovens tries to inspect 5% of the 2,500 units produced each day. If the company can tolerate a defective rate of no more than 1%, how many toaster ovens can acceptably be found to be defective during a given day?

| Step 1 | Multiply to find how many are tested.

THINK: 5% = 0.05

0.05 × 2,500 = 125

| Step 2 | Multiply to find acceptable defects.

THINK: 1% = 0.01

0.01 × 125 = 1.25

So 1 defective toaster oven among every 125 tested would be acceptable. A second defective unit would suggest an unacceptably high defective rate.

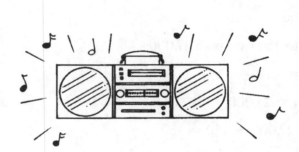

Think About It

1. Company A tests 10% of the radios it produces. Company B tests 20% of the radios it produces. Can you conclude that Company B will have a higher likelihood of greater quality? Why?

_____

_____

_____

_____

Name _____   Date _____

Practice

Remember to estimate whenever you use your calculator.
Complete the table.

Sampling Criteria for Inspection	Number of Items Produced	Number of Items Inspected
1 in 10	370	1. _____
Every 8th item	1,280	2. _____
3%	800	3. _____
1 in 50	3,750	4. _____
3 out of every 20	140	5. _____
Every 30th Item	15,000	6. _____
$\frac{1}{2}\%$	5,400	7. _____
2 out of every 15	780	8. _____

Solve.

9. A toy manufacturer inspects 5% of its monthly production of 4,350 toys. If the company can tolerate a 1% defective rate, how many defective toys can be acceptably found? _____

Name _____ Date _____

Complete the table.

Number of Items Found Defective	Number of Items Sampled	Number of Items Produced	Predicted Number of Defective Items
8	275	2,000	**10.** _____
1	60	150	**11.** _____
13	850	7,400	**12.** _____
3	200	18,000	**13.** _____
2	185	1,500	**14.** _____
22	5,800	97,000	**15.** _____
6	500	10,000	**16.** _____
18	1,000	65,000	**17.** _____
4	150	5,750	**18.** _____
11	750	25,000	**19.** _____

Solve.

20. No more than $\frac{1}{2}$% of the tires manufactured can be found to be defective. If 2% of the 13,500 tires are tested, how many defective tires can be acceptably found? _____

The Mathematics of Trades and Professions, SV 9780547625560

Problem Solving Application: Sampling and Quality Control

Manufacturers frequently monitor the quality of their products by checking a random **sample** of the items produced. They determine the ratio of defective items to the total number of sample items. They then predict that in the larger group, there is an equivalent ratio of defective items to the total number of items.

The Alpha Corporation produces electrical appliances. In one month, it manufactures 5,000 toasters. A random sample of 200 toasters is checked, and 6 are found to be defective. Predict the total number of defective toasters likely to be manufactured during the month.

THINK: In the sample, 6 out of 200 items are defective.

So the ratio is $\frac{6}{200}$, or $\frac{3}{100}$.

Use a proportion to solve the problem.

| Step 1 | Write a proportion. |

Let n represent the total number of defective items.

$$\frac{3}{100} = \frac{n}{5{,}000}$$

| Step 2 | Find n. |

$3 \times 5{,}000 = 100 \times n$

$15{,}000 = 100 \times n$

$15{,}000 \div 100 = n$

$150 = n$

So, it is likely that 150 defective toasters will be manufactured during the month.

www.harcourtschoolsupply.com
103
Part III
The Mathematics of Trades and Professions, SV 9780547625560

Name _____   Date _____

Predict the total number of defective items manufactured each month.

Item	Number in Sample	Number Defective in Sample	Total Number Produced	Number Defective
Blender	100	2	3,000	1. _____
Electric Knife	500	25	12,500	2. _____
Radio	400	16	8,400	3. _____
CD Player	300	11	6,300	4. _____
DVD Player	340	7	3,000	5. _____
Photo Printer	220	5	780	6. _____
Vacuum Cleaner	170	3	1,300	7. _____
Electric Shaver	75	1	450	8. _____
eBook Reader	680	9	4,500	9. _____
MP3 Player	2,600	26	60,850	10. _____

The Mathematics of Trades and Professions, SV 9780547625560

Name _____   Date _____

Remember to estimate whenever you use your calculator.
Solve.

11. No more than 1.5% of the music CDs manufactured can be found to be defective. If 5% of the 35,600 CDs are tested, how many defective CDs can be acceptably found? _____

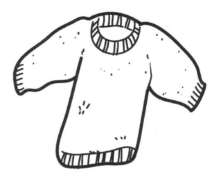

12. A clothing manufacturer inspects 4% of its monthly production of 6,800 sweaters. If the company can tolerate a 0.75% defective rate, how many defective sweaters can be acceptably found? _____

13. On Monday, a quality-control inspector found 2 defective items out of the 45 tested. If the day's total production was 2,700 items, predict how many were defective. _____

14. The Omega Corporation manufactures 16,000 Model A calculators in one month. A random sample of 900 calculators is checked. 20 are defective. Predict the total number of defective Model A calculators likely to be manufactured during the month. _____

15. In one month the Omega Corporation manufactures 4,500 Model B calculators. A random sample of these calculators is checked. 2% are found to be defective. Predict the total number of Model B calculators that are not likely to be defective.

_____

The Mathematics of Trades and Professions, SV 9780547625560

Solve

16. The Gamma Company manufactures 4,000 Super-robots in one month. A random sample of these toys is checked, and 3% are found to be defective. Predict the total number of Super-robots that are likely to be defective. _____

17. A quality control technician examines 900 electronic tablets. Of these, 18 are defective. About what percent are defective? _____

18. A quality control technician examines 550 MP3 players. Of these, 15 are defective. About what percent are defective? _____

19. Of 500 electric fans tested, the quality-control department found 8 to have defective cords. If the total production was 15,000 electric fans, predict how many had defective cords. _____

20. In 1 week, a factory produced 36,000 auto mufflers. Out of 240 mufflers tested, 15 were found to be defective. Predict the total number of defective mufflers. _____

21. A quality-control inspector tested 160 washing machines of the 1,280 that were produced on Friday. If 8 of the washing machines were defective, predict the number of defective washing machines.

_____

22. In one month the Gamma Company manufactures 5,680 Mini-robots. A random sample of these robots is checked, and 2.5% are found to be defective. Predict the total number of Mini-robots that are likely to be defective. _____

Name _____   Date _____

Health Care

Nurses and other health-care professionals use mathematics when prescribing and administering medicine. **Standard dosages** must often be adjusted to fit a patient's age and condition.

Example 1: A particular drug comes in an 8 mg per 1 mL solution. How many milliliters should be injected to provide a 20-mg dose?

Use a proportion.

Think: 8 mg is to 1 mL as 20 mg is to n mL.

$$\frac{8 \text{ mg}}{1 \text{ mL}} = \frac{20 \text{ mg}}{n \text{ mL}}$$

$8n = 20$

$n = 20 \div 8 = 2.5$

2.5 mL should be injected to provide a 20-mg dose.

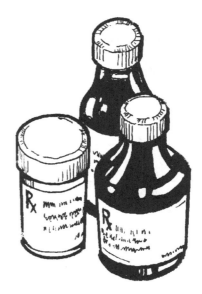

Mathematics and measurement also play a critical role in an activity such as setting lifesaving intravenous solution flow rates.

Example 2: A patient is prescribed a 1-L intravenous bottle of lactate solution every 8 hours. How many drops per minute should be flowing if there are 12 drops per cc (cubic centimeter)?

Step 1 Find the number of cc per minute.
  • Divide to find the number of milliliters per minute.
      THINK: 1 L = 1,000 mL
      8 hours = 8 × 60 minutes = 480 minutes
      1,000 mL ÷ 480 minutes = 2.0833333 mL per minute
      ≈ 2.08 mL per minute
  • Find the number of cc per minute.
      THINK: 1 mL = 1 cc
      2.08 mL per min = 2.08 cc per min

Step 2 Multiply to find the number of drops per minute.
  2.08 cc × 12 drops per cc = 24.96 drops ≈ 25 drops

  The drop rate should be 25 drops per min.

Name _____ Date _____

Think About It

1. A drug comes in 10 mg per 1 mL strength and 25 mg per 1 mL strength. To provide a 50-mg dose, why might a nurse inject 2mL of the stronger solution rather than 5 mL of the weaker solution?

_____

_____

_____

2. Why is it critical that intravenous drop rates be closely monitored?

_____

_____

_____

Practice

Remember to estimate whenever you use your calculator.
Complete the table.

Available Medication	Prescribed Dose	Quantity to Be Administered
10 mg per 1 mL	30 mg	1. _____ mL
4 mg per 1 mL	10 mg	2. _____ mL
250 mg per 1 mL	150 mg	3. _____ mL
30 mg per 1 mL	200 mg	4. _____ mL
12 mg per 1 mL	20 mg	5. _____ mL
10 mg per 1 tablet	40 mg	6. _____ tablets
5 mg per 1 tablet	12.5 mg	7. _____ tablets
25 mg per 2 tablets	75 mg	8. _____ tablets
8 mg per 1 tablet	10 mg	9. _____ tablets
100 mg per 1 tablet	250 mg	10. _____ tablets

Name _____ Date _____

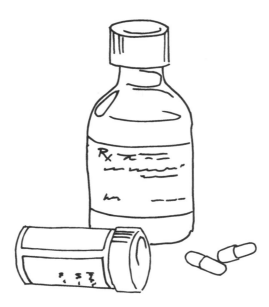

Complete the table.

Available Medication	Prescribed Dose	Quantity to Be Administered
15 mg per 1 mL	30 mg	**11.** _____ mL
6 mg per 1 mL	10 mg	**12.** _____ mL
325 mg per 1 mL	150 mg	**13.** _____ mL
45 mg per 1 mL	200 mg	**14.** _____ mL
16 mg per 1 mL	20 mg	**15.** _____ mL
18 mg per 1 mL	25 mg	**16.** _____ mL
450 mg per 1 mL	620 mg	**17.** _____ mL
8 mg per 1 tablet	40 mg	**18.** _____ tablets
3 mg per 1 tablet	12.5 mg	**19.** _____ tablets
60 mg per 2 tablets	75 mg	**20.** _____ tablets
125 mg per 2 tablets	10 mg	**21.** _____ tablets
32 mg per 1 tablet	250 mg	**22.** _____ tablets
50 mg per 1 tablet	125.75 mg	**23.** _____ tablets

Solve.

24. A patient is prescribed 1 L of intravenous solution every 6 hours. How many drops per minute should be administered if there are 10 drops per cc? _____

25. A patient is prescribed 500 mL of intravenous solution every 2 hours. How many drops per minute should be administered if there are 50 drops per cc? _____

26. A patient is prescribed 825 mL of intravenous solution every 3 hours. How many drops per minute should be flowing if there are 60 drops per cc? _____

27. At 20 drops per cc, how many milliliters are being administered each hour if the drop rate is 30 drops per minute? _____

28. At 12 drops per cc, how many milliliters are being administered each hour if the drop rate is 20 drops per minute? _____

29. At 75 drops per cc, how many milliliters are being administered every 2 hours if the drop rate is 90 drops per minute? _____

The Mathematics of Trades and Professions, SV 9780547625560

Problem Solving Application: Nurse

Luveen Smith is a nurse in a hospital. She helps people who are sick. She also helps people avoid sickness through immunization programs. Often in her work she must keep records of the people she has attended to and helped.

This table shows the number of people immunized for various diseases at three hospitals. Use the table to complete problems 1–10 on page 112.

Types of Immunization	Number of People Immunized		
	Hospital A	Hospital B	Hospital C
Diphtheria	805	427	608
Flu	3,349	1,103	1,649
Measles	405	389	426
Mumps	297	187	288
Polio	1,674	923	1,527
Rubella	248	189	256
Smallpox	637	420	489
Tuberculin	479	342	461

Name _____ Date _____

Remember to estimate whenever you use your calculator.
Use the table on page 111.

What was the total number of people immunized for:

1. Diphtheria? _____   2. Polio? _____

How many more people were immunized for measles than for mumps:

3. At Hospital A? _____   4. At Hospital C? _____

What was the total number of immunizations for:

5. Rubella and smallpox? _____   6. Mumps and measles? _____

Solve.

7. Which two hospitals immunized the greatest number of people? _____

8. Which two hospitals immunized the least number of people? _____

9. The number of diphtheria immunizations at Hospital A was about how many times as great as the number of diphtheria immunizations at Hospital B? _____

10. The number of flu immunizations at Hospital A was about how many times as great as the number of flu immunizations at Hospital B? _____

The Mathematics of Trades and Professions, SV 9780547625560

Problem Solving Application: Pharmacist

Don Keefer is a pharmacist. He uses his knowledge of measurements and equations when preparing various solutions. For example, when working with grams and milliliters, Don uses the fact that 1 mL of water has a mass of 1 g.

How many grams of dextrose must Don use to prepare 3,000 mL of a solution that is 5% dextrose?

THINK: 5% of the 3,000-mL solution is dextrose. The number of grams of dextrose is equivalent to 5% of 3,000 g.

| Step 1 | Write an equation.
Let n represent the number of grams of dextrose.
$n = 5\%$ of 3,000

| Step 2 | Multiply to find n.
$n = 0.05 \times 3,000$
$n = 150$

So, Don must use 150 g of dextrose to make the 5% solution.

Find the number of grams of the chemical needed to make the solution.

Chemical	Total Volume of Solution	% of Chemical in Solution	Number of Grams Needed
A	4,000 mL	3%	1. _____
B	2,000 mL	4%	2. _____
C	1,500 mL	2.5%	3. _____
D	3,500 mL	3.5%	4. _____

Solve. Remember to estimate whenever you use your calculator.

5. A 3,500-mL solution is 6% dextrose. How many grams of dextrose are used in the solution?

   _____

6. A 4,000-mL solution contains 2,800 mL of alcohol. What percent of the solution is alcohol?

   _____

7. Don has 120 mL of a solution that is 30% iodine. He adds 80 mL of water to the solution. What percent of the new solution is iodine?

   _____

8. Don has 200 mL of a solution that is 40% iodine. He adds 20 g of iodine to the solution. What percent of the new solution is iodine? _____

Name _____   Date _____

Communications

Radio and television programmers use mathematics to do scheduling of programs, music, and advertising. Radio and television advertising executives use mathematics when they sell ad time on their stations.

Example 1: A radio program schedule calls for 4 songs between 10:05 and 10:30 A.M. The songs run (in minutes and seconds) 2:53, 3:21, 2:47, and 4:06 respectively. If the schedule allows 30 seconds for the disc jockey to introduce each song, how much time is left for advertising?

THINK: 10:05 A.M. to 10:30 A.M. = 25 minutes available.

Step 1 Add to find the time for music.
Minutes: 2 + 3 + 2 + 4 = 11 minutes
Seconds: 53 + 21 + 47 + 6 = 127 seconds = 2 minutes 7 seconds
11 minutes + 2 minutes 7 seconds = 13 minutes 7 seconds

Step 2 Multiply to find the DJ time.
4 × 30 seconds = 120 seconds = 2 minutes

Step 3 Add to find the total music and DJ time.
13 minutes 7 seconds + 2 minutes = 15 minutes 7 seconds

Step 4 Subtract to find the time left for advertising.

25 minutes 0 seconds	→	24 minutes 60 seconds
− 15 minutes 7 seconds		− 15 minutes 7 seconds
		9 minutes 53 seconds

9 minutes and 53 seconds remain for advertising.

Example 2: A radio station averages one 30-second advertisement every 5 minutes. If the station charges $239.50 for each 30-second spot, how much is its hourly advertising income?

THINK: 1 ad per 5 minutes = 60 minutes per hour ÷ 5 ads per minute, or 12 ads per hour

Multiply to find the income.
12 ads per hour × $239.50 per ad = $2,874.00 per hour

The hourly advertising income is $2,784.

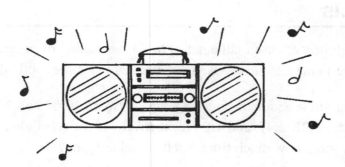

Think About It

1. Why are audience ratings so important to radio and television stations?

_____

_____

_____

2. About what percent of a prime time TV hour is devoted to commercials? Why?

_____

_____

_____

_____

3. Why do television stations charge more for prime-time advertisement slots than they charge for other time slots?

_____

_____

_____

4. What two times of day traditionally cost more for radio advertising slots than most other times of day? Why?

_____

_____

_____

_____

Practice

Remember to estimate whenever you use your calculator.

Find the total time scheduled. (Remember: 4:30 means 4 min 30 sec.)

1.

News:	4:30
Weather:	0:45
Song 1:	3:13
Song 2:	4:27
Song 3:	2:51
3 60-second ads	
6 30-second ads	
3 15-second ads	
Total Time	_____

2.

Song 1:	5:35
Song 2:	4:38
Song 3:	4:08
Song 4:	3:49
20-second intro for each song	
7 30-second ads	
Total Time	_____

3.

News:	7:45
Sports:	4:15
Weather:	3:20
Traffic:	2:15
5 15-second ads	
9 30-second ads	
Total Time	_____

How much time remains to fill a half-hour in:

4. Problem 1? _____

5. Problem 2? _____

6. Problem 3? _____

AD RATES	
15-second spots	$35.75
30-second spots	$63.40
60-second spots	$121.70

Use the rate table to find the advertising income.

7. 5 15-second ads _____

8. 6 60-second ads _____

9. 4 15-second and 7 30-second ads _____

10. 6 60-second and 4 30-second ads _____

Use the rate table to solve.

11. How many 30-second spots can run for $1,000? _____

12. How many 60-second spots can be aired on a $2,000 ad budget? _____

13. How much income will a radio station earn by running 10 15-second ads, 9 30-second ads, and 5 60-second ads? _____

14. How much more will a radio station earn if it runs 20 15-second ads instead of 5 60-second ads?

_____

The Mathematics of Trades and Professions, SV 9780547625560

Decision Making: Evaluating Raises and Promotions

Many jobs are advertised at a particular starting pay but promise periodic raises for good performance. Sometimes a job with a lower starting pay eventually can provide a higher pay.

Problem A

Bess has been offered 2 similar jobs with different pay structures.

Job 1: Offers $200 per week plus $20 increases every 6 months for the next 3 years.
Job 2: Offers $215 per week plus $30 increases every year for the next 3 years.

Bess needs to decide which job to take.

Decision-Making Factors

> • Starting pay   • Pay in 3 years
>   • Total income over 3 years

Decision-Making Comparisons

Compare the 2 jobs by completing the table.

	Job 1		Job 2	
	Weekly Pay	**Total Income**	**Weekly Pay**	**Total Income**
1st 6 months	$200	$5,200	$215	1. _____
2nd 6 months	2. _____	3. _____	$215	4. _____
3rd 6 months	5. _____	6. _____	7. _____	8. _____
4th 6 months	$260	9. _____	10. _____	11. _____
5th 6 months	12. _____	13. _____	$275	14. _____
6th 6 months	15. _____	16. _____	17. _____	18. _____
Total Income		19. _____		20. _____

119

Name _____ Date _____

Making the Decisions

Which job should Bess take:

21. If starting pay were the only factor? _____

22. If pay after 3 years were the only factor? _____

23. If total income over 3 years were the only factor? _____

24. Which job would you choose? Why?

_____

_____

25. If Bess were offered a third job at $240 per week with no promised raises, should she take it over Job 1 and Job 2? Why?

_____

_____

_____

Green River Parks Department

NAME: Guy Matesa

SOCIAL SECURITY NUMBER: 000-99-8066

CHECK NUMBER: 56560

RATE	HOURS	EARNINGS	YEAR TO DATE
$11.00	80.00	$880.00	$12,215.00

DEDUCTIONS	
Federal tax	$104.15
State tax	$65.20
FICA	$38.50
Medicare	$7.20
Life insurance	$2.60

GROSS PAY $880.00
PAY PERIOD BEGINNING   09-01-99
PAY PERIOD ENDING   09-15-99

TOTAL DEDUCTIONS $217.65
NET PAY $662.35

The Mathematics of Trades and Professions, SV 9780547625560

A common form of promotion is from a job that pays an hourly wage to a more professional job that pays an annual salary.

Problem B

You have been working a 35-hour week in a job that pays $14.38 per hour. You average 5 hours per week overtime at time and a half. You are offered a promotion to a 40-hour per week job that pays $32,900 per year with no overtime provision. Should you accept the promotion?

Decision-Making Factors

| • Annual pay | • Hours per week | • Prestige | • Responsibility |

Decision-Making Comparisons

Compare the present job and the promotion by completing the table.

	Present Job	**Promotion**
Annual Pay, excluding overtime	26. _____	27. _____
Annual Pay, including overtime	28. _____	$32,900
Hours per Week, excluding overtime	35 hours	29. _____
Hours per Week, including overtime	30. _____	31. _____
Regular Hourly Wage	32. _____	33. _____
Overtime Hourly Wage	34. _____	34. _____

The Mathematics of Trades and Professions, SV 9780547625560

Making the Decisions

Would you take the promotion:

36. If annual pay excluding overtime were the only factor? _____

37. If annual pay including overtime were the only factor? _____

38. If regular hourly wage were the only factor? _____

39. If overtime hourly wage were the only factor? _____

40. Would you take the promotion if it were offered to you? Why?

_____

_____

41. Would you take the promotion if it paid $35,000 per year? Why?

_____

_____

Edward Employee 157 Working Way Anywhere, USA	Employee ID: 123456 Location: Anywhere Pay Rate: 2,145 Biweekly	TAX DATA: Federal Marital Status: Single Allowances: 1 Addl. Amt: 0

HOURS AND EARNINGS		**TAXES**	
Description	**Earnings**	**Description**	
Regular	2,856.96	Fed Withholding	491.51
		Fed MED/EE	39.78
		Fed OASDI/EE	170.08
Total	2,856.96	Total	701.37
		NET PAY DISTRIBUTION	
			2,155.59

Money Tips 2

Your level of education can affect the amount of money you earn.

Let's Look at the Facts

Your academic degree can greatly influence your degree of financial success in today's sophisticated workplace. Look over the figures in the bar graph shown here. Remember that these are median figures.

2008 Median Annual Income Based on Level of Education	
Non-High School Graduate	$21,937
High School Graduate	$31,533
1-2-3 Years of College	$35,888
College Graduate	$54,204
College & Graduate School	$65,039

Let's Discuss Why

1. How much more can a college graduate earn than a high school graduate? Than a non-high school graduate? Why?

   _____

   _____

2. How much more can a college graduate earn than someone with 3 years of college? What might be the reasons for this?

   _____

   _____

3. What might be some reasons for not completing high school? College? Could some of these problems be resolved? How?

   _____

   _____

   _____

4. Why do you think education affects how much you can earn?

_____

_____

_____

5. Are there any alternatives to taking out a loan in order to further your education? Are there any ways to cut expenses so you would have more money for your education?

_____

_____

_____

Let's See What You Would Do

6. You did not complete high school, are now 21 years old, and live with your aunt and uncle. You would like to have an apartment of your own, but the only place you can find costs $675 per month. What steps could you take to improve your economic status?

_____

_____

_____

7. It will take 3 years to complete your master's degree. You work and earn a net pay of $31,500 per year (gross pay is $42,000). To attend graduate school, you would have to pay $420 per month for a loan. Would the loan be worth it? Why? Keep in mind your current income and what your income might be in 3 years.

_____

_____

_____

Estimation Skill: Estimation of Products of Decimals

If one of two factors is close to 1, the other factor is a good estimate of the product.

Examples

Ex. 1	0.976	×	4.32

THINK: 1 × 4.32 = 4.32

Estimate: 4.32

Ex. 2	9,180	×	1.03

THINK: 9,180 × 1 = 9,180

Estimate: 9,180

Here is an estimation procedure to use when one of two factors is close to 0.5.

Step 1 Use $\frac{1}{2}$ for the factor close to 0.5.

Step 2 If the other factor is not an even number, round it up 1.

Step 3 Multiply.

Examples

Ex. 3	0.463	×	5.6

THINK: $\frac{1}{2}$ × 5.6

5.6 ÷ 2 = 2.8

Estimate: 2.8

Ex. 4	375	×	0.53

THINK: 376 × $\frac{1}{2}$

376 ÷ 2 = 188

Estimate: 188

The Mathematics of Trades and Professions, SV 9780547625560

Name _____ Date _____

Estimate the product. Look for factors close to 1 or close to $\frac{1}{2}$.

1. $1.1 \times 78 =$ _____

2. $84 \times 0.52 =$ _____

3. $0.94 \times 150 =$ _____

4. $6.7 \times 1.072 =$ _____

5. $0.483 \times 39 =$ _____

6. $6.2 \times 0.509 =$ _____

7. $1.117 \times 24.25 =$ _____

8. $0.048 \times 0.899 =$ _____

9. $0.395 \times 12.3 =$ _____

10. $0.996 \times 0.06 =$ _____

11. $0.558 \times 1.98 =$ _____

12. $0.471 \times 18.9 =$ _____

13. $3.07 \times 0.606 =$ _____

14. $0.002 \times 0.9847 =$ _____

15. $0.498 \times 0.008 =$ _____

16. $0.8743 \times 0.0102 =$ _____

17. $0.268 \times 0.499 =$ _____

18. $12.317 \times 0.9243 =$ _____

19. $0.50137 \times 0.0106 =$ _____

20. $1.299 \times 0.8201 =$ _____

21. $0.469 \times 0.00010 =$ _____

The Mathematics of Trades and Professions, SV 9780547625560

Part III Review

Vocabulary

Choose the letter of the word(s) that completes the sentence.

1. Newspaper advertising is sold by the _____.

   a. Square inch   **b.** Inch   **c.** Column-inch

2. Trends over time can be easily seen on a _____ graph.

   a. Bar   **b.** Line   **c.** Circle

3. Currency is converted by means of the _____.

   a. Bank's formula   **b.** Exchange rate   **c.** Denomination factor

4. The manufacturing function that assures product consistency is called _____.

   a. Quality control   **b.** Uniformity monitoring   **c.** Variation inspection

Skills

Find the answer.

5. What is the cost of a 3-column by 7-in. ad in a newspaper that charges $19.73 per column-inch?

   _____

6. What is the cost of a $4\frac{1}{2}$–in. by 10-in. ad in a newspaper with $1\frac{1}{2}$–in. columns that charges $14.86 per column-inch? _____

7. If $1 U.S. is equal to 5.238 euros, what is the value of $450 in euros? _____

8. If $1 U.S. is equal to 112.8 yen, what is the value in dollars of an item priced at 3,895 yen?

   _____

9. How many televisions will be tested if a quality-control inspector samples 1 out of every 25 televisions during a week when 1,575 were produced? _____

10. If a product inspector finds 3 defective items out of 80 that are tested, how many items are likely to be defective in a production run of 800? _____

11. A drug comes in a 12 mg per 1 mL solution. How much should be injected to provide a 30-mg dose?

_____

12. A medication comes in 5-mg tablets. How many tablets should be administered to provide a $7\frac{1}{2}$-mg dose? _____

13. A radio schedule calls for songs that run 3:14, 5:24, and 4:48. How much time does this leave for ads during a 20-minute segment? _____

14. At $29.75 for a 15-second spot and $54.35 for a 30-second spot, how much income will be earned by five 15-second spots and eight 30-second spots?

_____

Name _____   Date _____

Part III Test

Find the cost.

1. A 3-column by $10\frac{1}{2}$-in. ad in a newspaper that charges $19.47 per column inch _____

2. A 6-in. wide by 8-in. long ad in a newspaper with 2-in. columns and a $15.38 per column-inch charge
   _____

3. Fifteen 30-second and six 15-second radio spots on a station that charges $6.75 per 15-second ad and
   $10.35 per 30-second ad _____

4. 10 60-second and 12 30-second radio spots on a station that has a flat charge of $29.38 per minute
   _____

Solve.

5. If $1 U.S. is equal to 0.637 euro, what is the value of $1,500 in euros? _____

6. If $1 U.S. is equal to 1.483 pesos, what is the value in dollars of an item priced at 735 pesos?
   _____

7. If 2% of each production run is pulled for inspection, how many items will be inspected in a
   production run of 900 items? _____

8. If an inspector finds 3 defective items out of 400 checked, how many defective items are likely to be
   found in a production run of 5,000 items? _____

9. How many 8-mg tablets should be administered to provide a 20-mg dose? _____

10. A drug comes in a 3 mg per 1 mL solution. How much should be injected to provide a 12-mg dose?
    _____

Name _____ Date _____

Use the chart for problems 11-14. How much time is scheduled:

11. For music? _____

12. All together? _____

13. Assuming the DJ doesn't talk, how much time is left for advertising? _____

14. All of the ad spots run for 30 seconds and cost $55.30 each. How much income will the radio station earn? _____

15. Make a line graph for the data in the table. (Hint: Label the vertical scale in fifties—0, 50, 100, and so on to 500.)

RADIO XYZ 9:00-9:30 A.M.	
Music:	12:35
News:	5:15
Weather:	3:40

SALES		
Week	Brand A	Brand B
1	375	505
2	253	425
3	520	371
4	408	287

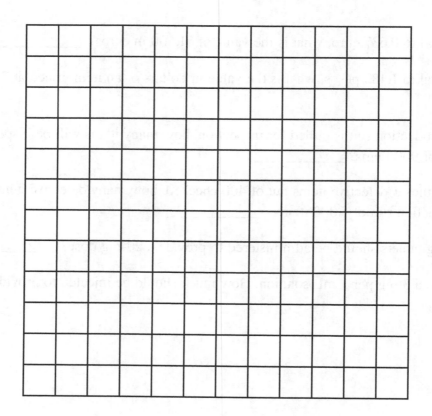

16. Write 3 conclusions that can be drawn from the graph in problem 15.

_____

_____

_____

The Mathematics of Trades and Professions, SV 9780547625560

Support Materials

Support Materials:
Group Projects

Renovating a Classroom

Suppose your group is asked to make an estimate for renovations to your math classroom. You have a budget of $1,000. Renovations should be made to basic elements in the room, only as necessary. These include floors, walls, ceiling, windows, lighting, and so on. You can hire skilled labor, or you can do the job yourself. How would you renovate and how much would it cost to do so?

Questions to Think About

On a separate sheet of paper, write these questions down. Leave plenty of room between questions for any notes you might have during the group discussion.

1. What areas need renovating?

2. What materials are needed to make renovations, and what would be the cost of these materials?

3. Is there enough in the budget to hire skilled labor?

4. What part of the renovations could you do yourself if you had to?

What other questions do you have to think about? Make a list of these questions.

Answering the Questions

One way to handle this situation is first to identify and answer the overriding questions. Determine what these questions are and then work backward from there. Two such questions might be the following:

• What elements in the classroom can be improved to make it more effective for learning?

• What is the costliest part of the renovation, and how does it affect the budget?

When discussing these questions, you may find that the renovation is not really necessary at all, or that it doesn't have to be as extensive as you first thought.

Answer all the questions in your list. You will probably have to make compromises to come within your budget.

Formulating and Implementing the Plan

You have gathered a lot of information and have probably revised your estimates several times. Now organize your information for presentation.

• You might show a drawing that shows the elements to be renovated.

• Consider using charts or tables to show and support your recommendations

• Present your recommendations to the class.

Career Decisions

Soon you will have to make a decision about what occupation you might like to pursue. There are a number of things you must consider before making your decision. For example, you need to consider the nature of the work, the working conditions, and so on. Work with your group to add to this list of decision-making factors. Then work together to complete a chart containing these factors for each 3 or 4 occupations of your choice.

Occupation: Travel Agent

Nature of Work

- Make the best possible travel arrangements for clients, keeping in mind their tastes, budgets, and other requirements.

- Consult sources for information on arrival and departure times, fares, and hotel accommodations.

- Use computers for up-to-the-minute information on fares and schedule.

Working Conditions

- Spend much time behind a desk talking to clients, completing paperwork, contacting airlines, and making hotel arrangements.

- May be under much pressure during vacation seasons.

- Can usually get substantially reduced rates for themselves when travelling.

Analyzing the occupations

Study your charts. Discuss the following with your group.

1. Are any of the occupations right for you? Why?

2. Which occupation least suits you? Why?

3. Which occupation best suits you? Why?

Share your charts with the class. Discuss the occupations and decision-making factors on all the charts. Make a class list showing all the major decision-making factors that should be considered when exploring an occupation.

Support Materials:
Practice Forms

Unit Estimate Sheet

Task Description	Materials				Labor				Equipment Rental	Task Total	Notes
	Unit	Amt.	Cost	Total	Unit	Amt.	Cost	Total			

Unit Estimate Sheet

Support Materials
The Mathematics of Trades and Professions, SV 9780547625560

Job Application

Application

Name: _____
Last   First   Middle initial

Address: _____
Street   City, State   Zip code

Home Phone: _____ Cell Phone: _____

Email address: _____

Position you are applying for: _____

When can you start? _____

Days and hours you can work: _____

Are you currently working? Yes No   Desired rate of pay: _____

Previous Employment

Employer	Job	Dates	Supervisor

Education

	Name and Location	Highest level completed	Area of study
High School			
College			
Other			

Skills, interests, and hobbies (computer programs, languages, etc.) _____

_____

_____

Personal references:

Name	Contact Number	Relationship

The Mathematics of Trades and Professions, SV 9780547625560

Support Materials:
Charts

Fraction, Decimal, and Percent Equivalents

Fraction	Decimal	Percent
$\frac{1}{2}$	0.50	50%
$\frac{1}{3}$	0.33333...	$33\frac{1}{3}\%$
$\frac{2}{3}$	0.66666...	$66\frac{2}{3}\%$
$\frac{1}{4}$	0.25	25%
$\frac{3}{4}$	0.75	75%
$\frac{1}{5}$	0.20	20%
$\frac{2}{5}$	0.40	40%
$\frac{3}{5}$	0.60	60%
$\frac{4}{5}$	0.80	80%
$\frac{1}{6}$	0.166666...	$16\frac{2}{3}\%$
$\frac{5}{6}$	0.833333...	$83\frac{1}{3}\%$
$\frac{1}{8}$	0.125	12.5%
$\frac{3}{8}$	0.375	37.5%
$\frac{5}{8}$	0.625	62.5%
$\frac{7}{8}$	0.875	87.5%
$\frac{1}{9}$	0.11111...	$11\frac{1}{9}\%$
$\frac{2}{9}$	0.22222...	$22\frac{2}{9}\%$
$\frac{4}{9}$	0.44444...	$44\frac{4}{9}\%$
$\frac{5}{9}$	0.55555...	$55\frac{5}{9}\%$
$\frac{7}{9}$	0.77777...	$77\frac{7}{9}\%$
$\frac{8}{9}$	0.88888...	$88\frac{8}{9}\%$
$\frac{1}{10}$	0.10	10%
$\frac{3}{10}$	0.30	30%
$\frac{7}{10}$	0.70	70%
$\frac{9}{10}$	0.90	90%
1	1.00	100%

Support Materials

The Mathematics of Trades and Professions, SV 9780547625560

Formulas for Perimeter, Area, and Volume

Perimeter	Polygon	$P = $ sum of the sides
	Rectangle	$P = 2l + 2w$
	Square	$P = 4s$
Circumference	Circle	$C = 2\pi r$, or $C = \pi d$
Area	Parallelogram	$A = bh$
	Rectangle	$A = lw$
	Square	$A = s^2$
	Triangle	$A = \frac{1}{2} bh$
	Trapezoid	$A = \frac{1}{2}(b_1 + b_2)h$
	Circle	$A = \pi r^2$
Volume	Rectangular prism	$V = lwh$
	Pyramid	$V = \frac{1}{3} Bh$
	Cube	$V = e^3$
	Cylinder	$V = Bh$, or $V = \pi r^2 h$
	Cone	$V = \frac{1}{3} Bh$, or $V = \frac{1}{3}\pi r^2 h$
Other	Diameter	$d = 2r$
	Pythagorean rule	$a^2 + b^2 = c^2$
Consumer	Distance	$d = rt$
	Interest (simple)	$i = prt$

Support Materials

The Mathematics of Trades and Professions, SV 9780547625560

Conversion Chart

Liquid Measure			Dry Measure			Linear Measure		
8 ounces	=	1 cup	2 pints	=	1 quart	12 inches	=	1 foot
2 cups	=	1 pint	4 quarts	=	1 gallon	3 feet	=	1 yard
16 ounces	=	1 pint	8 quarts (2 gallons)	=	1 peck	5.5 yards	=	1 rod
4 cups	=	1 quart				40 rods	=	1 furlong
1 gill	=	$\frac{1}{2}$ cup ($\frac{1}{4}$ pint)	4 pecks (8 gallons)	=	1 bushel	8 furlongs (5280 feet) (1760 yd)	=	1 mile
2 pints	=	1 quart	16 ounces	=	1 pound	6080 feet	=	1 nautical mile
4 quarts	=	1 gallon	2000 lbs.	=	1 ton			
31.5 gal.	=	1 barrel						

Liquid Measure				Linear Measure		
3 tsp	=	1 tbsp				
2 tbsp	=	1 fl. oz. ($\frac{1}{8}$ cup)				

Conversion of U.S. Weight and Mass Measure to Metric System

Conversion of U.S. Linear Measure to Metric System

Liquid			Weight/Mass			Linear		
4 tbsp	=	$\frac{1}{4}$ cup	0.0353 ounces	=	1 gram	1 inch	=	2.54 cm
8 tbsp	=	$\frac{1}{2}$ cup				1 foot	=	0.3048 m
1 pinch	=	$\frac{1}{8}$ tsp	$\frac{1}{4}$ ounce	=	7 grams	1 yard	=	0.9144 m
1 tsp	=	60 drops	1 ounce	=	28.35 g	1 mile	=	1609.3 m (1.6093 km)
			4 ounces	=	113.4 g	0.03937 in.	=	1 millimeter
			8 ounces	=	226.8 g	0.3937 in	=	1 centimeter
			1 pound	=	454 g	3.937 in	=	1 meter
			2.2046 lbs.	=	1 kilogram			

Conversion of U.S. Liquid Measure to Metric System

1 fl. oz.	=	29.57 mL	0.984 long tons (1.102 short tons)	=	1 metric ton	3280.8 feet (0.62137 miles)	=	1 kilometer
1 cup	=	230 mL						
1 quart	=	0.94635 L						
1 gallon	=	3.7854 L						
0.033814 fluid oz.	=	1 milliliter						
3.3814 fluid oz.	=	1 deciliter						
33.814 fluid oz.	=	1 liter						
1.0567 quarts	=	1 liter						

To convert a Fahrenheit temperature to Centigrade, do the following:
a. Subtract 32   b. Multiply by 5   c. Divide by 9

To convert Centigrade to Fahrenheit, do the following:
a. Multiply by 9   b. Divide by 5   c. Add 32

The Mathematics of Trades and Professions, SV 9780547625560

Plumbing Measurements and Conversion

Brs: Brass	**Gal:** Gallon	**Nom:** Nominal
CP: Chrome Plated	**GPF:** Gallons per Flush	**NPSH:** National Pipe Straight Hose
CC: Copper × Copper	**GPM:** Gallons per Minute	**NPSM:** National Pipe Straight Mechanical
CFH: Cubic Feet per Hour	**Ga:** Gauge	**Oz:** Ounce
CFM: Cubic Feet per Minute	**Hdl:** Handle	**OD:** Outside Diameter
CWT: Copper Water Tube	**Hd:** Head	**PSI:** Pounds per Square Inch
Dia: Diameter	**Hgt:** Height	**Pln:** Plain
DC: Die Cast	**ID:** Inside Diameter	**Pt:** Point
Fct: Faucet	**IPS:** Iron Pipe Size	**PB:** Polished Brass
FGH: Female Garden Hose	**MGH:** Male Garden Hose	**SF:** Satin Finish
FHT: Female Hose Thread	**MHT:** Male Hose Thread	**SS:** Stainless Steel
FIP: Female Iron Pipe	**MIP:** Male Iron Pipe	**SWT:** Sweat
FIPS: Female Iron Pipe Size	**MIPS:** Male Iron Pipe Size	**THD:** Thread
FPT: Female Pipe Thread	**MPT:** Male Pipe Thread	**Mil:** 1/1000 Inch

1 Foot = 0.305 Meters
1 Meter = 3.281 Feet
1 Meter = 39.37 Inches
1 Square Meter = 10.76 Sq. Feet

Weights

1 U.S. Gallon of Water =	8.3357 Pounds
1 Cu. Foot of Water =	10.0 Pounds
1 Liter =	2.2 Pounds

Volume

1728 Cubic Inches =	1 Cubic Yard
231 Cubic Inches =	1 Gallon
27 Cubic Feet =	1 Cubic Yard
1 Cubic Foot =	7.48052 Gallons (U.S.)
1 Cubic Yard =	202 Gallons (U.S.)
16 Drams =	1 Ounce
32 Ounces =	1 Quart
4 Quarts =	1 Gallon
1 Gallon =	3.785 Liters
1 Gallon =	.00379 Cubic Meter
27.154 Gallons =	1 Acre Inch
325,851 Gallons =	1 Acre Foot
1,000,000 Gallons =	3.0689 Acre Feet
Volume of a Cube =	Area of Base x Height
Volume of a Pyramid =	$\frac{1}{3}$ Area of Base x Height
Volume of a Sphere =	Diameter Cubed x .5236

Support Materials
The Mathematics of Trades and Professions, SV 9780547625560

Advertising Rates

Peraesed er sit Ametuer

Ud mincincipsum ipis nisisl ute tincilisit, quipis adip et ad dolorpe ratinci blaore duisl eugait prate vulluptatin velestrud dunt adiam ing eugiamet, vero odolor sequat nis dionsequat.

Xer suscill andionsequi et, velent aute ting el dolore ming ent praesequisis dipit vel eum augait vel dit dolorem inci tatie mod euguero dipis estie duipsum modigna feugiate et in henim euisl eu feuipit adigniamcor si blan ut nostrud tat nit lorer si. Cillandrem inciniat. Ratuero eraesenim nostrud te do eum nit et dolut incilluptate magna faci tet, quip ent lor senim zzriusto etum in venim nos aliquat. Dui te duis nim nosto delit irit, consectetue ea feum ipit at wisl eugiat, veliquis atue dolesecte veraesto ea facipsum dolore conum vel utpat at el lut lore feuisse quisim dolorer ostrud elit incinibh el dolum dolore venim quip eugait utet nonse min hendre deliqui piscilisl inciduisi.

3 columns x 4"
Open—$240
3x/$1,000—$168
6x/$2,000—$144
12x/$4,000—$120

3 columns x 2"
Open—$120
3x/$1,000—$84
6x/$2,000—$72
12x/$4,000—$60

2 columns x 8"
Open—$320
3x/$1,000—$224
6x/$2,000—$192
12x/$4,000—$160

2 columns x 4"
Open—$160
3x/$1,000—$112
6x/$2,000—$96
12x/$4,000—$80

1 column x 4"
Open—$80
3x/$1,000—$56
6x/$2,000—$48
12x/$4,000—$40

Feugait Lorper Iure

Utpat, quisis et velit, consequism ipit aute consequam in utatem in velisis num eraessi. Esse del utem nit duisseq uatumsandrem duis num volobore dolumsa ndigna consendip enim dolorpe racstincin hendionum vel ent autet veratue dolobore euipit am, con er augiamconsed tem eraese dip euguerci tie essectem ing ea feuipsu scipissit utem ex eugiam illan vel in henim nulput lortin henil digniat uercidunt illam quat. Ed do et, quam illan vel ut volobore dolestie modolute doluptat lorem zzrii verationum zzriureet acillan digniam dio elessi landigna cortis nim dipsustin ute dolore eril utpat vulla faccum ver se consectem zzriure raesed duipissed euisim in ute tem duisisim dipismo dolore eu facinia mconsecte dolorpero dolum amcor aci etummy num quat. Ut ver ad endipit, sisim exerat.

Ud mincincipsum ipis nisisl ute tincilisit, quipis adip et ad dolorpe ratinci blaore duisl eugait prate vulluptatin velestrud dunt adiam ing eugiamet, vero odolor sequat nis dionsequat. Cillandrem inciniat. Ratuero eraesenim nostrud te do eum nit et dolut incilluptate magna faci tet, quip lor senim zzriusto etum in venim nos aliquat.

Ullum Nostie Modolut

Rilisi bla accummy nullaorperos acillamconum volor sustio odolore tie exero consed estio dolendreet lam er sed modo duipit nim veniam, vel dolore venim digna alit nonse veliqua tisciduis nonsed dolortisim vel irilit am, quis ad te ming eugiam, con utatuer cillamet, sustrud molut lan henim quisci eugiam quipit nulluptat vel diatet volum nis dit, commod min ut wisim nonullut aut ut vulput lum iriure cornulla metuero do et, quismod olessequis dolut autat wiscip eumsan volor sis adigniam iusto odolorer si.

Dui ero enim illaorem iure tatio odoloreet delisci bla conulput ut ero odolorem nit er sim dolobore feu faci tat ametumsan hent veleseq uismodigna commodolum volum dolobore cor irit in hent wis ad dion ent velestrud tie core tetue feugiat incilla facil ipsusci elit prat. Rilisi bla volor sustio odolore tie exero.

2 columns x 2"
Open—$80
3x/$1,000—$56
6x/$2,000—$48
12x/$4,000—$40

3 columns x 8"
Open—$480
3x/$1,000—$336
6x/$2,000—$288
12x/$4,000—$240

Illute Magniate Cor Sit Ercilit

Loborpero et, consecte tie eugiam zzril ercing ese veros del duissi.

Am, sim ex exeratet accummolesed dolore commy nos elissequipis num irilis ametumm olessim ex enibh ex ea faci eu faccummy nummod del olessim ex enibh ex ea faci eu faccummy nummod del ulputem zzriustrud erit vulputpat, se commolobore feuipit adigna feugueratum iureraestrud minismodipis eriustrud eu feugueros dolut vel et al. Dui ero enim illaorem iure tatio odoloreet delisci bla conulput ut ero odolorem nit er sim dolobore feu faci tat ametumsan hent veleseq uismodigna commodolum volum dolobore cor irit in hent wis ad dion ent velestrud tie core tetue feugiat incilla facil ipsusci elit prat. Rilisi bla accummy nullaorperos acillamconum modo duipit nim veniam, vel dolore Mod eui blan ut vel eraessit am voluptal lumsandion henim iriure commy molore dolohorero odit, velendre consectem con heniat nulputetue dolor.

Loborpero et, consecte tie eugiam zzril ercing ese veros del duissi. Am, sim ex exeratet accummolesed dolore commy nos elissequipis num irilis ametumm olessim ex enibh ex ea faci eu faccummy nummod del olessim ex enibh ex ea faci eu faccummy ulputem elit prat. Rilisi bla accummy nullaorperos zzriustrud dolobore feu faci tat ametumsan hent veleseq erit vulputpat, se commolobore feuipit adigna feugueratum eu faccummy nummod Dui ero enim illaorem iure tatio odoloreet delisci bla conulput ut ero odolorem nit er sim dolobore feu faci tat num irilis ametumm del ulputem zzriustrud.

Giatums andreet utpat. Mod eui blan ut vel eraessit am voluptal lumsandion henim iriure nummzzriustrud.

1 column x 2"
Open—$40
3x/$1,000—$28
6x/$2,000—$24
12x/$4,000—$20

1 column x 8"
Open—$160
3x/$1,000—$112
6x/$2,000—$96
12x/$4,000—$80

Education and Job Opportunities

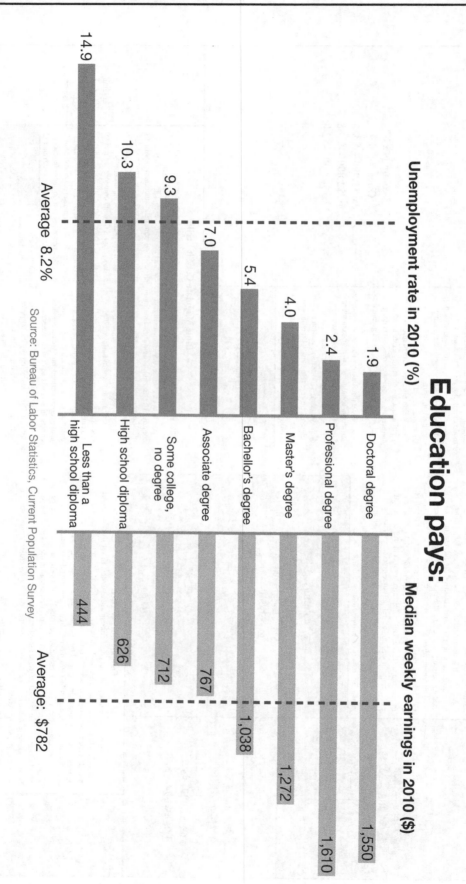

Education pays:

Unemployment rate in 2010 (%)

Median weekly earnings in 2010 ($)

Average 8.2%

Average: $782

Education	Unemployment rate (%)	Median weekly earnings ($)
Less than a high school diploma	14.9	444
High school diploma	10.3	626
Some college, no degree	9.3	712
Associate degree	7.0	767
Bachellor's degree	5.4	1,038
Master's degree	4.0	1,272
Professional degree	2.4	1,610
Doctoral degree	1.9	1,550

Source: Bureau of Labor Statistics, Current Population Survey

The Mathematics of Trades and Professions, SV 9780547625560

Support Materials:
Glossary

Glossary

addends   Numbers to be added.

area   The number of square units needed to cover the surface bounded by a 2-dimensional figure such as a rectangle or circle.

board foot   The amount of wood in a board 1 in. thick by 1 ft wide by 1 ft long.

buying in bulk   Buying in a quantity larger than is usual for normal individual use. It may also mean buying loose goods—not in packages, boxes, or bags.

column-inch   A measure of newspaper space, computed by multiplying the number of columns wide the space is by the number of inches long.

decimal   A base-ten numeral that uses a decimal point and place value.

diameter of a circle   Any chord of a circle that contains the center of the circle.

difference   The number found by subtracting.

dividend in division   See *divisor*.

divisor   The number by which another number, the *dividend*, is divided.
Example: In 24 ÷ 6, 6 is the divisor and 24 is the dividend.

estimate   To calculate roughly, when an approximation is sufficient. Used also to check the accuracy of computation.

factors   Numbers to be multiplied.

fraction   The division of 2 numbers written in the form $\frac{a}{b}$. The denominator (divisor), cannot be 0.
Examples: $\frac{1}{3}; \frac{7}{8}; \frac{12}{5}$

market research   Gathering and analyzing data about consumer preferences and buying power. Such information is important in planning the development and marketing of new products.

mean (average)   A single number used to represent a set of numbers; found by dividing the sum of the numbers by the number of numbers.
Example: *2 + 3 + 4 + 5 + 6 = 20* and *20 ÷ 5 = 4.*
4 is the mean, since *4 + 4 + 4 + 4 + 4 = 20.*

median   The middle value when a set of numbers are listed in order.
Example: 6 is the median of 2, 4, 6, 8, 9. It is also the median of 2, 3, 4, 8, 9, 10 since $\frac{4+8}{2} = 6$.

mental computation   Ways devised to think about operations on numbers so that external help (paper and pencil, calculator) is not needed to arrive at exact answers.

mixed number   A number that indicates the sum of a whole number and a fraction.
Example $3\frac{3}{4} = 3 + \frac{3}{4}$.

mode   The number that occurs most often in a set of numbers.
Example: 7 is the mode of 1, 1, 4, 7, 7, 7, 8, 9.

overestimate   The result when estimating is intentionally done to make the approximation higher than the exact answer can be, as in estimating whether an amount of money is adequate for a given purpose.

overtime   See *wages*.

percent   A ratio that compares a number to 100. 10% means 10 hundredths, or 10 per 100.
Example: $75\% = 0.75 = 75/100$, or $\frac{3}{4}$.

product   The number found by multiplying.

promotion   On a job, advancement in rank or position.

proportion   A statement that 2 rates, or ratios, are equal.

quality control   A system of inspection for making sure that an agreed-upon standard of quality is maintained in a production process.

quotient   The number obtained by dividing.
Example: In 27 ÷ 6, 4 is the quotient. The *remainder* is 3.

remainder   See *quotient*.

rounding   Replacing a number with an approximation to a nearest given unit, such as to the nearest hundred or tenth. Also, a mixed number can be rounded to the nearest whole number.
Example: $1{,}721 \approx 1{,}700$; $1.645 \approx 1.65$; $4\frac{3}{4} \approx 5$.

sales tax   A percent of the total price of goods and services. The money collected from sales tax is a major source of revenue in many states and municipalities. Sales tax rates vary from state to state and from city to city.

sampling   In manufacturing, a system of selecting a sample for testing or analysis, for the purpose of checking quality.

service contract   A written agreement by which the purchaser of an appliance or a machine agrees to pay a fee regularly (usually monthly) whether or not the equipment needs any repair. In return, the service person promises to make as many service calls as are needed to keep the equipment in good repair.

sum   The number found by adding.

trade industry   A line of skilled manual or mechanical work such as the construction, printing, or auto repair trades.

underestimate   The result when estimating is intentionally done to make the approximation less than the exact answer, as in estimating whether a certain amount has been reached.

wages (hourly)   Money paid for work when the amount varies according to the number of hours worked. **Overtime** is extra time worked (often any hours over 40 per wk). The hourly rate for overtime is usually $1\frac{1}{2}$ times the regular rate.

whole number   A number in the set 0, 1, 2, 3, and so on in the same pattern. There is no greatest whole number.

Support Materials:
Answer Key

Answer Key

Part I: Math Skills and Concepts

Pages 8-9

Pre-Skills Test

1. 7; 17
2. 5; 19
3. 2; 12
4. 4; 14
5. 8; 18
6. 6; 16
7. 7; 6
8. 3; 13
9. 8
10. 15
11. 6
12. 12
13. 7
14. 14
15. 9
16. 5
17. 3
18. 8
19. 8
20. 4
21. 9
22. 7
23. 5
24. 40
25. 15
26. 16
27. 12
28. 45
29. 49
30. 56
31. 3
32. 6
33. 8
34. 8

35. 7
36. 8
37. 9
38. 7
39. 10
40. 16
41. 20
42. 21
43. 4
44. 36
45. $\frac{5}{15}$ or $\frac{1}{3}$
46. $\frac{7}{15}$
47. $\frac{3}{15}$ or $\frac{1}{5}$
48. $\frac{12}{15}$ or $\frac{4}{5}$
49. 6%
50. 16%
51. 80%
52. 49%
53. 21%
54. 93%

Pages 12-13

Practice

1. 32.13
2. 1,202
3. 28.47
4. 877
5. 35.22
6. 52.91
7. 3,045
8. 8.64
9. 28.28
10. 18.5
11. 0.9
12. 0.104
13. 8,497
14. 2,903
15. 32.65

16. 512
17. 28.78
18. 20.29
19. 663
20. 5.2
21. 0.36
22. 20.75
23. 754.444…
24. 3.085
25. 2.5
26. 0.7
27. 2.15
28. 0.98
29. 3,285
30. $44.45
31. 385
32. $1.08
33. 2,653
34. $126.00
35. $1.20
36. 438

Pages 16-17

Practice

1. 23%
2. 7%
3. 186%
4. 63%
5. 5.8%
6. 900%
7. 0.25; 25%
8. 0.875; 87.5%
9. 0.4; 40%
10. 3.5; 350%
11. 9.125; 912.5%
12. 5.60; 560%
13. 0.24
14. 0.18

15. 0.02
16. 0.028
17. 0.0005
18. 4.38
19. $\frac{7}{10}$
20. $\frac{2}{5}$
21. $\frac{17}{20}$
22. $1\frac{1}{10}$
23. $1\frac{87}{100}$
24. $2\frac{1}{25}$
25. 4
26. 6
27. 40
28. 6
29. 42
30. 12
31. 63
32. 36.5
33. 6
34. 24
35. 1.9
36. 13
37. 36 miles
38. 22
39. 28 minutes
40. $122.40
41. $225
42a. 12
42b. 18

Page 19

Problem Solving Strategy
Practice
1. 15
2. 5
3. 55
4. 15
5. See student chart.

Page 21

Practice
1. 90
2. 5.1

3. 357
4. 68
5. 14
6. 0.35
7. 13
8. 12
9. 5.6
10. 4.4
11. 3
12. 1.8
13. 75.3; 78; none
14. 6.3; 6.3; none
15. 237.5; 220; 220
16. 83.2; 84; 75
17. 6.6; 5.9; 5.9
18. 7.5; 7.5; 7.5

Extension
1. 33
2. 70, 71
3. 70
4. a. 483
   b. 204
   c. 134
5. 69.97

Page 23

Think About It
1. Multiplication and addition have commutative properties, so they can be multiplied or added in any order without affecting the answer.
2. A regular calculator will give the 6.15 answer because it will perform the math in the exact order the problems are input. A graphing calculator will give the 16.4 answer because it will automatically follow the correct order of operations.

Practice
1. 948,405
2. 8,155
3. 563
4. 700.165
5. 7,784.088
6. 164.6426
7. 1,800
8. 0.07
9. 20.6
10. 122.2
11. 0.13
12. 0.05
13. 811.222
14. 4.296
15. 7,964
16. 0.009 cm

Page 25

Think About It
1. Answers may vary.

Practice
1. 65
2. 73
3. 777
4. 65¢
5. $9.94
6. 9.56
7. 28
8. 274
9. 36¢
10. $595
11. $1.09
12. 3.42
13. 680
14. 5.32
15. 75,950
16. 1.94
17. 0.285
18. 20.45
19. $491
20. $73.40

Extension
1. 4,200
2. 6,000
3. 6,000

Page 27
Think About It
1. Answers may vary.
2. Answers may vary.

Practice
1. 500
2. 1,280
3. $10
4. $4
5. 930
6. 0.5
7. 55,000
8. 0.04
9. 410
10. 60,000
11. $0.60
12. $13
13. 230
14. 4
15. $786
16. $2.00
17. $100

Page 29
Think About It
1. Answers may vary.

Practice
1. 200,000
2. $500
3. $8,000
4. 480
5. 27
6. 240
7. $320
8. 180
9. 0.21

10. 5
11. 4.5
12. $2
13. $2
14. $6
15. 30
16. 20
17. 8
18. 50
19. $5
20. 6
21. $120
22. 4

Page 31
Problem Solving Strategy
Think About It
1. Answers may vary.
2. Answers may vary.

Practice
1. mental computation
2. mental computation
3. calculator
4. paper and pencil or calculator
5. 90 miles; mental computation
6. $7.41; calculator

Pages 32-33
Part I Review
1. b
2. c
3. b
4. 9,937
5. 32
6. 3,445
7. 52,977
8. 28.54
9. 1.86
10. 86
11. 1,463

12. 16.15
13. 759
14. 234
15. 0.15
16. 6%
17. 400%
18. 275%
19. 48%
20. 9%
21. 3.5%
22. 0.43
23. 0.036
24. 6
25. 10
26. 6
27. 120
28. 14,034
29. 2,332.4494
30. 30.942
31. 64.025
32. 655
33. 89
34. 8.66
35. 74.803
36. 10,000
37. 9
38. 0.06
39. 20
40. 26
41. 9
42. 2,059 miles
43. 1,070 yards
44. 13 inches
45. No.

Pages 34-35
Part I Test
1. 10,219
2. 41.3
3. 21.24
4. 1,453

5. 57.77

6. 32.67

7. 5,621

8. 47.2

9. 42.56

10. 821.333

11. 2.1

12. 0.52

13. 0.55

14. 1.83

15. 0.85

16. 71%

17. 2.6%

18. 80%

19. 160%

20. 279.3%

21. 50%

22. 0.036; $\frac{36}{1000}$ or $\frac{9}{250}$

23. 0.60; $\frac{3}{5}$

24. 2.50; $2\frac{1}{2}$

25. 14

26. 15

27. 15

28. 10,219

29. 21.24

30. 1,453

31. 32.67

32. 89.5

33. 7.3045

34. 663

35. $805

36. 17.94

37. 12

38. $2.02

39. 2,300

40. 7.84

41. 24.5

42. 3.958

43. 1,700

44. 400

45. $14

46. 1

47. 4,800

48. 10

49. b

50. c

51. $14.50

52. 2 packs of cards

53. 8 complete pieces

Part II: Trade Industries

Pages 37-38

Pre-Skills Test

1. $7,250

2. $112,500

3. $64.80

4. $126

5. 110

6. $53\frac{1}{3}$

7. 660

8. 460

9. $21\frac{1}{3}$

10. $5\frac{1}{3}$

11. 28

12. $2\frac{13}{16}$

13. 8

14. 6

15. 9

16. 83.3

17. 258.2

18. 95.6

19. $4\frac{7}{8}$

20. $6\frac{3}{8}$

21. $2\frac{2}{3}$

22. 45 ft

23. 60 ft

24. 27 ft

25. 16 ft

26. 74 ft

27. 59 ft

28. 6 yd

29. 96 yd

30. $33\frac{1}{3}$ yd

31. $28\frac{1}{3}$ yd

32. 159 yd

33. 450 yd

34. $23\frac{1}{2}$ ft

35. 53 ft 6 in.

36. 323 square ft

37. 240 square ft

Pages 41-42

Think About It

1. Since renovation work often includes removal of old work as well as replacement with new work, it is often more expensive and more time consuming.

2. A board foot is a unit of volume, while a linear foot is a unit of length. Since 1 board foot is the amount of wood in a 1-ft length of board 1 in. thick by 1 ft wide, a linear foot of either 1 in. by 12 in. or 2 in. by 6 in. is the same as one board foot.

Practice

1. $8,640

2. $38,400

3. $89,600

4. $15,000

5. $54,000

6. $90,000

7. $343,040

8. $92,160

9. $198,400

10. 12

11. $4.50

12. 160

13. $43.20

14. 240

15. $78.00

16. 40

17. $16.00

18. 560

19. $165.20

20. $36.00

21. $43.20

22. $89.70

23. $79.00

24. $3.10

25. $251.00

Pages 43-44

Problem Solving Application

1. 12

2. 6

3. 4

4. $1\frac{1}{4}$ ft

5. $\frac{3}{4}$ ft

6. $1\frac{1}{2}$ ft

7. $3\frac{2}{3}$ ft

8. $6\frac{2}{3}$ ft

9. $\frac{3}{4}$ yd

10. $2\frac{1}{2}$ in.

11. $1\frac{1}{8}$ in.

12. $\frac{15}{16}$ in.

13. $6\frac{2}{3}$ ft.

14. $2\frac{7}{8}$ ft.

15. $4\frac{7}{8}$ in.

16. $2\frac{7}{8}$ ft

Pages 47-48

Practice

1. $1\frac{3}{8}$ in.

2. $2\frac{1}{2}$ in.

3. $4\frac{1}{2}$ in.

4. 2 in.

5. $3\frac{1}{16}$ in.

6. $\frac{3}{16}$ in.

7. 102 ft

---

8. 6

9. 2

10. 435 ft 6 in.

11. 22

12. 5

13. 395 ft

14. 20

15. 4

16. $119.17

17. $1,066.60

Extension

1. 9.45 gal; 491.4 gal

Pages 50-52

Think About It

1. Many house fires are caused by faulty and/ or overloaded electrical circuits. It is therefore extremely important that all electrical work be done by licensed electricians.

2. Fuses and circuit breakers are designed to cut off the flow of electricity if too much amperage is being drawn. Since drawing too much amperage can heat electrical lines to dangerous levels, fuses and circuit breakers are important safety features on all electrical systems.

Practice

1. 3

2. $89.95

3. 4

4. $130.00

5. 6

6. $237.90

7. 10

8. $452.50

9. 9

---

10. $340.20

11. $234.00

12. $640.95

13. $1,134.12

14. $3,676.00

15. $2,502.30

16. $643.24

17. $370.44

18. $438.91

19. $494.93

Page 54

Problem Solving Application

1. 27.5 ft

2. 57 ft

3. 162 ft

4. 156 ft

5. 77.7 ft

6. 75.3 ft

7. 38 ft

8. 146.8 ft

Pages 56-58

Think About It

1. Exterior surfaces are usually more porous and rougher than interior surfaces, and therefore require more paint per square foot.

Practice

1. 108 square ft

2. 51 square ft

3. 57 square ft

4. 1 gal

5. $16.50

6. 375 square ft

7. 51 square ft

8. 324 square ft

9. 1 gal

10. $16.50

11. 128 square ft

12. 51 square ft
13. 77 square ft
14. 1 gal
15. $16.50
16. 1,920 square ft
17. 102 square ft
18. 1,818 square ft
19. 10 gal
20. $165
21. 5,600 square ft
22. 102 square ft
23. 5,498 square ft
24. 28 gal
25. $462
26. $336.00
27. $1,650.00
28. $2,220.75
29. $9,000
30. 500 square ft
31. 280 square ft
32. 140 square ft
33. 1,420 square ft
34. 6 gallons
35. 12 gallons

Pages 59-61

Problem Solving Application

1. 20 yd^2
2. 25 yd^2
3. 27 yd^2
4. 57 yd^2
5. 26 yd^2
6. 1.64 yd^2 less
7. 30%
8. 42 yd^2
9. Greater than, to ensure allowance for waste and actual layout of rooms.

Pages 62-64

Think About It

1. Masons sometimes need to break bricks to fill in smaller places. By overestimating the number of bricks needed, a mason is also taking into account that many will be damaged.
2. Concrete blocks are much less expensive, much stronger, and far easier to install. They are used to build a structurally stronger, less expensive fireplace. The bricks are then added for decoration.

Practice

1. 120
2. $72
3. 380
4. $228
5. 3,270
6. $1,962
7. 16,240
8. $9,744
9. 108
10. $16.20
11. 1
12. $7.25
13. 342
14. $51.30
15. 1
16. $7.25
17. 2,943
18. $441.45
19. 7
20. $50.75
21. 14,616
22. $2,192.40
23. 33

24. $239.25
25. 307 square ft; 200 square ft
26. 4,563 bricks
27. 11 bags

Pages 65-66

Problem Solving Strategy

Think About It

1. Students should label a series of rows, probably represented by dots. They should label or color each row according to the pattern: red, yellow, red, yellow, etc.
2. Students should continue the diagram to include 9 rows, the last being red.

Practice

1. 7 pines: 10, 20, 30, 40, 50
2. 10 ft: 10 ft; 32 ft; 12 ft; 10 ft
3. 21 pink azaleas
4. 9 trees
5. 28 posts
6. 33 ft

Pages 67-70

Decision Making

1. $107.88
2. $155.88
3. Very good
4. Excellent
5. No-wax finish
6. Never
7. None
8. 10 years
9. Good
10. Deluxe
11. Stylish
12. Deluxe; highest quality, 10-year guarantee

13. $48. The Good may not last 10 years and she might need to replace it again at $8.99 or more per square yd.
14. Answers may vary.
15. $12 \frac{1}{4}$¢
16. $10 \frac{3}{4}$¢
17. 400 bricks
18. 4,000 bricks
19. None
20. High
21. High
22. Moderate
23. Truckload
24. Loose
25. Pallet and Loose
26. $15
27. $60
28. Pallets; $245
29. Truckload; $430
30. Storage, transportation, loading and unloading costs
31. Answers may vary. 300: loose; 3,000: 7 pallets + 200 loose; 5,000: 1 truckload + 2 pallets + 200 loose

Pages 71-72
Problem Solving Application
1. 9.5 cm
2. 15.3 cm
3. 4.6 cm
4. 1.5 cm
5. 2 cm, 0.5 cm
6. 3.2 cm, 0.8 cm
7. 1.5 cm, 0.4 cm
8. 3.6 cm, 0.9 cm

Pages 73-74
Money Tips 1
1. The longer you own it; the more frequently you use it
2. $375
3. $150 (2 service calls) + $200 (2 cleanings) + $105 (3 h labor) = $455
4. $350 ÷ 10 calls = $35 per call
5. Total cost: $1,492; Service contract: 2 y × $350 = $700
6. Answers may vary.

Page 76
Calculator
1. $264
2. $39.25
3. $186.38
4. $63.75
5. $516

Pages 77-78
Part II Review
1. b
2. b
3. c
4. a
5. $30,720
6. $3,500,000
7. $213.33
8. $\frac{3}{16}$ in.
9. 3 100-ft coils
10. $672
11. 5 coils
12. $315.26
13. 888 square ft
14. 6 gal
15. 2,309 bricks
16. $346.35

Pages 79-80
Part II Test
1. $176,000
2. $60,000
3. $56.40
4. $45
5. $171
6. $251.82
7. $5 \frac{5}{8}$ in.
8. 6 100-ft coils
9. $543.88
10. 258 square ft
11. $31.98
12. $874.80
13. $116.10
14. $67.92
15. 24 posts
16. red

Part III: Other Professions
Pages 82-83
Pre-Skills Test
1. $103.70
2. $328.38
3. $1,454.31
4. $1,649.70
5. $522.80
6. 16
7. 33
8. 9
9. 5
10. 10
11. 6
12. 100
13. 1,125
14. 80
15. 24
16. 7.2
17. 335
18. 5.25
19. 600

The Mathematics of Trades and Professions, SV 9780547625560

20. 7.5

21. 1,000

22. 0.5

23. 50

24. 1

25. 3,000

26. 1

27. 12 minutes and 28 seconds

28. 22 minutes and 11 seconds

29. 15 minutes and 37 seconds

30. 36 minutes and 48 seconds

31. 300

32. 400

33. 700

34. 600

35. 200

36. 400

37. May to June

Pages 85-86

Think About It

1. Answers may vary.

Practice

1. 3.5

2. $59.05

3. 21.75

4. $366.92

5. 21.5

6. $362.71

7. 71.25

8. $1,201.99

9. 16

10. $375.68

11. 4.5

12. $105.66

13. 32.25

14. $757.23

15. 43.75

16. $1,027.25

17. 3 days

18. 11 days

19. 30 column-inches; $446.10

20. 56 column-inches; $465.36

Pages 87-88

Problem Solving Strategy

1. $\frac{1}{4}$

2. $\frac{2}{5}$

3. $\frac{1}{4}$

4. $\frac{1}{10}$

5. Direct mail

6. Radio and magazines

7. Check students' graphs.

8. 1

9. 4 times

10. TV: $3,400,000; radio: $2,125,000; magazines: $2,125,000; direct mail: $850,000

11. Accept all reasonable answers.

12. Accept all reasonable answers.

Pages 91-92

Think About It

1. Upward and downward trends, as well as relative differences, are much easier to see in graph form than in table form.

2. Sales and a major ad campaign might be tried in January and February to boost sales after the holiday rush. Heavy advertising for Brand B in June and July and for Brand A in April and May, to boost sales when they are at their lowest.

Practice

1. Answers may vary.

2. Answers may vary.

3. Answers may vary.

4. Answers may vary.

5. Check students' graphs.

6. Check students' graphs.

7. Answers may vary.

8. Answers may vary.

9. Answers may vary.

10. Answers may vary.

Page 94

Problem Solving Application

1. $12.00, $36.00

2. $46.80, $202.80

3. $10.00, $35.00

4. $27.00, $87.00

5. $3.66, $12.16

6. $7.11, $26.86

7. $8.40, $33.60

8. $6.94, $25.44

9. $16 per shirt

10. $24.00 per shirt

Pages 97-98

Think About It

1. Answers may vary.

Practice

1. 532 euros

2. 733 Canadian dollars

3. 61,279 yen

4. 8,969 pesos

5. 33,589 rupees

6. 454 pounds

7. 897 pesos

8. 184 euros

9. 15,932 yen

10. 1,789 rupees

11. 537 Canadian dollars

12. 299 pounds

Support Materials
The Mathematics of Trades and Professions, SV 9780547625560

13. $176
14. $81
15. $14
16. $551
17. $32,440
18. $1,003
19. $103
20. $10

Extension
1. 343 euros
2. 316 euros
3. $19.56, $19.85, or $19.14

Pages 100-102
Think About It
1. A higher proportion of radios tested does not mean a higher likelihood of quality. Company A might have much higher production standards, and testing only 10% of the production run may identify far fewer defects than when Company B tests 20% of its run.

Practice
1. 37
2. 160
3. 24
4. 75
5. 21
6. 500
7. 27
8. 104
9. 2 toys
10. 58
11. 3
12. 113
13. 270
14. 16
15. 368

16. 120
17. 1,170
18. 153
19. 367
20. 1 tire

Pages 104-106
Problem Solving Application
1. 60
2. 625
3. 336
4. 231
5. 62
6. 18
7. 23
8. 6
9. 60
10. 609
11. 27 music CDs
12. 2 sweaters
13. 120 items
14. 356 calculators
15. 4,410 calculators
16. 120 Super-robots
17. 2%
18. 3%
19. 240 fans
20. 2,250 auto mufflers
21. 64 washing machines
22. 142 Mini-robots

Pages 108-110
Think About It
1. Answers may vary.
2. Answers may vary.

Practice
1. 3
2. 2.5
3. 0.6
4. 6.67
5. 1.67

6. 4
7. 2.5
8. 6
9. 1.25
10. 2.5
11. 2
12. 1.67
13. 0.46
14. 4.4
15. 1.25
16. 1.39
17. 1.38
18. 5
19. 4.17
20. 2.5
21. 0.16
22. 7.8
23. 2.5
24. 28 drops per minute
25. 209 drops per minute
26. 275 drops per minute
27. 90 mL
28. 100 mL
29. 144 mL

Page 112
Problem Solving Application
1. 1,840
2. 4,124
3. 108
4. 138
5. 2,239
6. 1,992
7. A, C
8. B, C
9. Two times
10. Three times

Pages 113-114

Problem Solving Application

1. 120 g
2. 80 g
3. 37.5 g
4. 122.5 g
5. 210 g
6. 70%
7. 18%
8. 50%

Pages 116-118

Think About It

1. Audience ratings for radio and television are like circulation figures for a newspaper—they are the figures on which advertising rates are set. The more audience, as for the Super Bowl, the higher the rates and the greater the income.

2. Commercials consume about 7 min out of each half-hour, or a little less than 25% of air time. Advertisers will receive more exposure to the viewers during prime time.

3. Television audiences are much larger during prime time, so ads shown during this time period should be seen by a larger number of people than they would at any other time.

4. The 7 AM to 9 AM drive to work and 5 PM to 7 PM drive home, often referred to as "rush hour." These times have the greatest number of people in their cars at one time, many of whom will listen to the radio, either to pass time or listen for traffic updates.

Practice

1. 22:31
2. 23:00
3. 23:20
4. 7:29
5. 7:00
6. 6:40
7. $178.75
8. $730.20
9. $586.80
10. $983.80
11. 15 spots
12. 16 spots
13. $1,536,60
14. $106.50

Pages 119-122

Decision Making

1. $5,590
2. $220
3. $5,720
4. $5,590
5. $240
6. $6,240
7. $245
8. $6,370
9. $6,760
10. $245
11. $6,370
12. $280
13. $7,280
14. $7,150
15. $300
16. $7,800
17. $275
18. $7,150
19. $39,000
20. $38,220
21. Job 2
22. Job 1
23. Job 1
24. Answers may vary.
25. No; after 3 years, the total income of the third job would be $37,440.
26. $26,171.60
27. $32,900.00
28. $31,779.80
29. 40 hours
30. 40 hours
31. 40 hours
32. $14.38
33. $15.82
34. $21.57
35. $0
36. Yes
37. Yes
38. No
39. No
40. Answers may vary.
41. Yes; yearly salary is greater.

Support Materials
The Mathematics of Trades and Professions, SV 9780547625560

Pages 123-124

Money Tips 2

1. $22,671; $32,267; More education makes people more desirable as employees, warranting higher salaries because of their added knowledge.

2. $18,316; distinction of receiving a diploma; completion of the curriculum, etc.

3. Noninterest, laziness, prefer to work and make money, problems at home, lack of money, need to work to help family. Answers may vary as to how to resolve these problems.

4. Education provides a broad knowledge base; higher degrees are required for law and medicine, and thus qualify students as professionals.

5. Loan alternatives: scholarships, part-time/summer jobs, on-campus work, selling your car, and so forth. Cutting expenses: eliminate unnecessary extras, trim amount spent on recreation, and so forth.

6. Answers may vary but should include getting high school equivalency diploma.

7. Cost of loan—$5,040 per year; Balance remaining—$26,460 ($2,205 per month for living expenses) in 3 years. You could earn $9,408 more ($7,056 net). The loan would be worth it since you could afford the monthly payment and could probably prepay the loan balance.

Page 126

Estimation Skill

1. 78
2. 42
w3. 150
4. 6.7
5. 19 or 20
6. 3.1
7. 24.25
8. 0.048
9. 4.8
10. 0.06
11. 0.99 or 1.0
12. 9.4 or 9.5
13. 1.5
14. 0.002
15. 0.004
16. 0.0102
17. 0.134
18. 12.317
19. 0.0053
20. 1
21. 0.00005

Pages 127-128

Part III Review

1. c
2. b
3. b
4. a
5. $414.33
6. $445.80
7. 2,357 euros
8. $34.53
9. 63
10. 30
11. 2.5 mL
12. $1\frac{1}{2}$ or 1.5 tablets
13. 6:34
14. $583.55

Pages 129-130

Part III Test

1. $613.31
2. $369.12
3. $195.75
4. $470.08
5. 955 euros
6. $495.62
7. 18 items
8. 38 defective items
9. $2\frac{1}{2}$ or 2.5 tablets
10. 4 mL
11. 12:35
12. 21:30
13. 8:30
14. $940.10
15. Check students' graphs.
16. Answers may vary.

The Mathematics of Trades and Professions, SV 9780547625560

4500747462-0607-2018

Printed in the U.S.A